HELEN BRADLEY'S LANCASHIRE

Helen Bradley's
LANCASHIRE

TEXT BY

INA TAYLOR

HALSGROVE

IN ASSOCIATION WITH

HELEN BRADLEY PRINTS LTD

First published in 2002 by Halsgrove
Text and Images © 2002 Helen Bradley Prints Ltd

British Library Cataloguing-in-Publication Data
A CIP record for this title is available from the British Library

ISBN 1 84114 214 X

HELEN BRADLEY PRINTS LTD
25 Silverwell Street
Bolton BL1 1PP
T: 01204 386676
F: 01204 386608
www.helenbradley.co.uk

Publishing and sales enquiries:
HALSGROVE
Halsgrove House
Lower Moor Way
Tiverton, Devon EX16 6SS
T: 01884 243242
F: 01884 243325
www.halsgrove.com

Printed and bound in Italy by Centro Grafico Ambrosiano

Contents

Acknowledgements

The author would like to thank the following people for their help in the preparation of this book:

Mr Peter Bradley, the late Mr Thomas Bradley, Mrs Jane Durrant, Mrs Elizabeth Morton, the late Mrs Dorothy Wilde and other members of Helen Bradley's family who have been so supportive throughout.

I am also grateful to Mr Michael D Abrahams, Mr S N Boler, Mr David Brunnschweiler, Clarke Art Limited, Mr David Eaves, Mrs Raena Green, Richard Green, Mr Bert M Kirshner, M G Fine Art Limited, W H Patterson Fine Art Limited, Mr Geoffrey Shyrane, Dr Leonard Steinberg, Mrs Lorraine Stones, Mrs Annabel Watts, Miss Kathryn Whittingham and Mr Stephen Whittle who helped in the preparation of this book in so many different and valuable ways.

Especial thanks are due to Keith and Patricia Lee of Miss Carter Publications (25 Silverwell Street, Bolton BL1 1PP) whose unswerving support for Helen Bradley and her work over the past thirty years has culminated in this celebration of her life and art.

Introduction

The charm of Helen Bradley's art lies in her blend of nostalgia and homeliness. Unlike many artists who write or paint scenes from childhood, Helen Bradley actually becomes the child again. She re-lives events and sees them through a child's eyes, rather than simply looking back as an adult. This results in a wonderful sense of fun in her pictures; this is life without any pretensions – children sort out a private quarrel behind the fence as a funeral goes by, or someone runs out with a bucket and shovel to collect the offerings from a passing horse and cart, or the Christmas party is shown where 'our Billy' wet his pants.

Her pictures have an exquisite attention to detail. You can stand for hours gazing and find so much to study: the interior of the front room with a dresser full of china, two dogs tugging at a hair ribbon under the table, or an assignation by the window. If that were not joy enough, many of the characters in Helen Bradley's pictures reappear in other pictures to continue the story, so her art has all the fascination of a long-running serial. Before long we are caught up in another episode. Will Miss Carter gain the longed-for proposal of marriage? Helen Bradley, the consummate storyteller, has ensnared us!

Her art captures that optimism and vibrancy felt at the dawn of the Edwardian period after the dark sobriety of the Victorian era. Helen Bradley's street scenes and processions positively teem with life and her figures are painted in glowing colours.

The public loved Helen Bradley's work when it was first seen in 1965 and were intrigued to discover the artist was a lady, aged sixty-five, who had had limited art training and only started painting these pictures late in life. The media had a field day; they adored her. The 'jolly granny', they called her. 'England's own Grandma Moses', 'The pensioner who started painting' and 'Success at sixty-five' were some of the headlines. The art of Helen Bradley was launched and exhibitions followed in Britain, America and even Japan.

Helen herself was quite bemused by all the fuss. She had simply painted her view of the first decade of the twentieth century to show her grandchildren what life was like then. Far from being chocolate-box scenes of rural England, this is urban life without any frills but much gentle humour. Helen Bradley's world was the small industrial town of Lees, on the northern fringe of Oldham in Lancashire. This was a place where the skyscape was dominated by smoking mill chimneys, creating polluted air and a strangely coloured light. The townscape was defined by rows of back-to-back houses. Most of the local population wore clogs and shawls, or braces and working clothes. Theirs was a hard existence with scant opportunity for holidays and pleasure.

Helen's paintings record a small town in transition. Horse transport predominated and there were still cottage industries; local women made and sold sweets from their back kitchen. But as Helen recalled, 'Mother would never allow us to have the most delicious of all sweets, Martha Higginbottom's chewy egg and milk toffee, because she put the pans of this sweet on the stone floor to cool and, having four or five cats, they used to prowl around the cooling tins and wait for the egg and milk to be sufficiently cool enough to lick.' At the same time there was industrialisation. Most of the town's inhabitants were employed in the cotton industry, particularly in the mills that overshadowed the town. The 'electric' tram had reached Lees and the appearance of the occasional motor car in the High Street caused a flurry of excitement. There was just as much interest in the arrival of the first indoor flush water closet.

Although life for many of Lees' inhabitants was barely above subsistence, they made the most of the opportunities that presented themselves. Helen painted the street pageants such as the Whit Parade, the procession with a brass band, or the impressive funeral of a local tradesman, in an era when a good send-off was all important.

Helen Bradley's world is not a bleak one. Whilst acknowledging things were hard for most people at the time, she took delight in the incidents that gave colour to people's lives – the escaping bull that ran down the main street, the mill fire or the suffragettes' march. And then there was her own family.

Helen's personal world was that of the middle-class trademan's family, effectively the aristocracy of Lees. In her pictures and stories she captured the essence of their lives, particularly the women of the family. These were individuals who were fortunate enough not to have to earn their living, who could indulge their interest in fashion and local gossip. Helen, a child at the time, was the observer and for decades she stored away in her memory those images and stories.

All her life she had wanted to paint and made various attempts to get started but it was only when she put the two together – the art and the childhood — that she discovered her talent, and the world of Helen Bradley was born.

Today Helen Bradley is recognised as a major naïve artist of the twentieth century, Britain's equivalent to the American Grandma Moses. Her subject matter is idiosyncratic and her painting techniques unconventional. The result? A sheer delight, accessible to everyone and loved by thousands.

Mercury Gallery Dec 1966

Helen Bradley

Helen Bradley was born Nellie Layfield on 20 November 1900 in Lees, Lancashire. Because this was a musical family, she was christened Nellie in honour of Dame Nellie Melba, the great soprano Helen's father admired. Helen, however, hated the name Nellie and preferred people to believe her proper name was Helen; in 1974 she changed her name from Nellie to Helen by deed poll.

In the family she was known affectionately as Nellie Bly after the skipping rhyme:

> *Nellie Bly caught a fly*
> *Tied it to a string*
> *Let it out to fly about*
> *But couldn't get it in.*

Years later when she began painting, Helen signed her landscapes Helen Layfield, even though she was married, but when the pictures were of her own family, she was reluctant to put her name to them. Instead she painted a small fly in the corner. The fly is visible on

Mother and Helen as baby

many of these early pictures (like the one on page 24). From around 1971 her paintings (like page 31) carried a signature, which might be Helen Layfield Bradley or Helen Bradley, plus the fly.

Helen was the eldest of four children born to Jane Shaw and her husband Frederick Layfield. Both Shaws and Layfields were lower middle-class families, well regarded by most of the neighbourhood because both families were owners of small businesses. Their trades were intimately bound up with the life-blood of the area – wool and cotton. The Shaw family were tailors and the Layfields hosiers. It comes as no surprise that Helen's work should reflect the families' obsession with clothes and fashion. These things mattered because new clothes were regarded as a status symbol at the time. Only people with money bought new clothes; the vast majority of the population of Lees bought their garments from one of the many market stalls selling second-hand clothes, whereas Helen's father walked out of a Sunday afternoon resplendent in top hat and tails, attended by his wife in silk dress and magnificent hat. The most notable of mother's hats, Helen recalled, had a bird of paradise from New Guinea perched on it. This made such a big impression on Helen that later it was the one she decided to paint on the head of Miss Carter.

On Helen's paternal side, the Layfields were headed by Grandfather Joe, who had a reputation for ingenious inventions to improve machinery used in the hosiery trade. It was said he had been to America in the 1880s and 90s to advise the Singer Sewing Machine Company. By the time Helen was born, Grandfather Layfield had retired to Blackpool, although he still maintained business interests in the Lees area through his warehouses. Some of his wealth and trade had been settled on his sons, who included Helen's father Freddie.

Grandfather Layfield had taken up fatherhood again in his retirement, with the youngest Layfield, Edith, only three years older than Helen. The two girls were playmates when Helen stayed with her grandparents. Edith features in a few of Helen's pictures of her childhood but, as so often, Helen uses some artistic licence. In the painting 'Aunt Edith was seventeen and wept for love' a little six-year-old Helen watches her aunt as a young girl crying over a boy in 1910. The reality was that in 1910, Helen was ten and Edith thirteen, and they attended school together when Helen stayed for a long holiday in Blackpool that summer. Holidays with the Layfield grandparents in Blackpool were a highlight of childhood. The excitement of catching the train to Blackpool, coupled with seaside scenes and even cricket matches, all provided a rich quarry of material for her later. Memories of winter expeditions to the farms near Blackpool also featured, because it was their custom to go and collect the Christmas ducks for various family dinner tables.

Despite the delightful interludes provided by visits to the Layfield grandparents, it was Helen's mother's family, the Shaws, who featured most prominently in her childhood and played leading roles in her art. Grandmother Shaw, with two unmarried daughters, Aunts Fanny and Mary, lived on the opposite side of Lees High Street to Helen at number 67. Their home, a large double-fronted stone house, was also the premises of David Shaw & Son – tailors, whose wares were displayed in one of the bow windows. The other bow window, suitably net-curtained, enabled Grandmother and the Aunts (as they were almost always called) to keep up-to-date with happenings in the High Street without being seen.

Grandfather David Shaw, like most of Helen's male relatives, rarely featured in her pictures, although he too lived in the house opposite. He was a prosperous businessman and a local dignitary who had been chairman of Lees Council. It was thanks to Shaw's efforts, in particular, that the inhabitants of Lees gained the modern 'electric tram' service running up to Lees from Oldham, and Grandfather was photographed in all his finery proudly riding on one of the inaugural runs of this new horseless tramcar. Ironically, perhaps, he died in 1908 after being trampled by a runaway horse startled whilst pulling the milk cart. 'Somehow we didn't miss Grandpa very much,' Helen said, relieved the God-fearing old man, with piercing blue eyes and a penchant for spouting Old Testament passages, now rested in the graveyard. Instead there were weekly family outings to Grandfather's grave which were to furnish Helen with a new subject for her art. She may not have had much regard for him, but her mother and the Aunts had cause to be grateful to David Shaw; he settled comfortable sums of money on all his daughters.

Grandmother Shaw's house can be recognised in the background of many of Helen's street scenes by the characteristic series of long windows on the third floor, which were designed to give hand-loom weavers maximum light. Sometimes Helen depicts 'The Loom House', as it was called, as one property and sometimes as two in her pictures, but there is no mistaking the house. The unusual top floor in the house, where she was allowed to play on condition she did not touch anything, stuck in her memory:

Two large looms were always in use there. Maggie Knott, who was very old, came to weave the cotton or linen sheets on one. Aunt Mary had the other loom and in her spare time wove yards of woollen cloth for winter coats, or fine pieces for frocks, just as Mother or the Aunts required them. She loved weaving and we loved watching her. She wove lovely colours and Mother and Aunt Frances would discuss at great length what they would make with it. The cloth when it was, woven had to be taken to Huddersfield to be pressed and finished.

Maggie Knott, the aged crone who held a weird fascination for children, provided a subject for one of Helen's portraits of her. (See page 79)

The house where Helen was born was just off the main street but shortly after her birth the family moved round the corner to be virtually opposite Grandmother's in Lees High Street. Their house was similar to many others in the street and one of several properties owned and rented out by Grandfather Shaw. Once again a family property was put at her parents' disposal. Although most of Helen's interior pictures are located in Grandmother's house, Helen set some domestic activities in her own home. 'Wednesday', a picture originally intended as a design for one of a set of decorative plates, shows their own kitchen with her mother baking bread. She also located scenes like 'Monday was the Great Wash Day' in their own backyard.

High Street Lees Courtesy Oldham Library

By using her own home as well as Grandmother's, Helen could extend not just her locations but also her regular cast of characters to include some of the daily helpers her mother employed.

Helen's childhood world was essentially a female one where men, like Father, Grandfather and uncles, were away at work and took no part in her daily life. The women of the households supervised the daily chores and had plenty of time for leisure activities. All was watched and overheard by the young Helen. As she explained, 'Children lived in a grown-ups' world in the 1900s and were not allowed to speak unless spoken to.' This had its advantages. All too often the adults forgot the presence of a silent child and chatted away about local gossip. Scraps of information and scandals overheard were to surface again sixty years later woven into stories and pictures. Most of Helen's pictures have a grain of truth in them but do not portray exact events. Like all artists, Helen used real life as a springboard for her creativity.

The Aunts, who took such leading roles on Helen's stage, were not quite as they appear in the pictures. In 1906, the year that features most frequently in Helen's work, Aunt Mary, the eldest, was a widow of thirty-seven who, after losing her only child, had returned home to live with her mother and teach at the elementary school, which Helen attended in Knowls Lane. Aunt Fanny, who also lived with Grandmother, was a spinster of thirty-six (Helen thought Fanny such a horrible name, that she calls her Aunt Frances in the stories although Fanny was her given name). The youngest of the Aunts, Charlotte, had died of tuberculosis a few years earlier. Helen's mother Jane, the youngest of the surviving sisters, was thirty. But it was the idea of a bevy of pretty young women in their early twenties, with a consuming interest in husband-hunting and the fashionable clothes that appeared in *The Queen* magazine, that inspired Helen Bradley's art. It is interesting to see the little real-life details that stuck in Helen's mind from those days reappearing in her paintings. The same lace-edged tablecloth seen in the photograph of the Aunts is visible in several scenes set in Grandmother's front room.

The search for husbands may well have dominated the conversation but the reality was that Aunt Fanny did not marry until 1922, when she was fifty-two, and her husband, James Alfred Buckley, sixty. Helen painted the lovers snatching a chance meeting in her picture 'Uncle John's Wedding'. Whether his mother really hindered the wedding, as Helen's accompanying story says, is not known, but by the time Aunt Fanny was ready to tie the knot Mr Buckley was a

The Aunts and Mother – note the tablecloth which can be seen on pages 67 and 120

wealthy man. 'Budnip', as he was nicknamed, made his fortune from a medicine he manufactured, patented and sold at his chemist shop in Lees High Street. 'Budnip Powders', a mixture of aspirin, ginger and oil of cinnamon, were reputed to cure all ills. When they proved successful enough for Beechams to buy him out, 'Budnip' was able to take Aunt Fanny as his bride and retire.

Helen did not remain an only child for long; brother George came along in 1903. He is seen in this photograph, along with Helen and his mother, dressed in bonnet and skirt like most Edwardian toddlers, male and female. George was Helen's bosom childhood companion and he appears in virtually all her paintings, frequently dressed in a sailor suit. Helen always took the lead, not only because she was the elder, but also the extrovert and the initiator of childish pranks.

Two more children followed in the Layfield family, Dorothy in 1907 and Arthur in 1910, but the gap between the first two children and the second two was significant.

Helen, George and Mother

George and Helen in fancy dress

Helen felt they were not a part of her childhood and consequently did not include them in the pictures she later painted. Once as a special present for her sister Dorothy, to whom she was close later in life, Helen painted Dorothy as a babe in arms, but her brother Arthur was never accorded that recognition.

Family life for the Layfield children centred around music; art had no place in their household. Helen's father was a keen musician and Sundays were devoted to music, not religion which he disdained. In the morning three of father's friends arrived at the house to make a string quartet in which Freddie Layfield played the violin. On Sunday evenings members of the Oldham Orchestral Society (founded by Freddie Layfield) were sometimes invited for supper with their wives. The music-making that followed was strictly a male activity with the men performing in the music room, whilst their wives occupied themselves with cups of tea and gossip in the sitting-room.

All the Layfield children were taught an instrument because their father liked to dream of a time when the whole family would perform as an ensemble. George and Dorothy were taught violin, Arthur cello and Helen the piano so she could be the accompanist. She enjoyed piano-playing, practised regularly and was considered by many to be an accomplished pianist. In addition to performing at home, the Layfield children were taken to concerts in Oldham to hear leading musicians such as Myra Hess and Gerald Moore. It is said that on one occasion Gerald Moore heard Helen play at home and was so impressed he urged Mr Layfield to consider letting his daughter take her music further. But a career in music, or in any other arena, was not part of her father's plan.

Art did find a place in Helen's young life thanks to the Shaw family. Grandfather Shaw had a younger brother, known to Helen as Great-Uncle Charles Shaw, who had seen his work hung at the Royal Academy on three occasions. Great-Uncle Charles's arrival in Lees always caused excitement in the family as Helen recalled:

When he came to the North to give an exhibition he would often stay with us – and how we all loved those visits – the comings and goings, getting pictures ready – having them all round our music room and discussing them. How he was going to hang them and the great thrill of the opening night.

Helen also remembered excursions on the moors with him:

Mother and the Aunts went for a walk and Great-Uncle Charles would set himself up for the day, setting up his easel and paints under a huge umbrella. He was such fun and an interesting and lovable person for any young person to be with. 'Look, Nellie Bly,' he would say, 'Just look at that lovely colour. Look at the sun glinting across that round grass. Or look at that tree how pink it looks against that dark cloud.'

Thinking back when she was famous herself, Helen felt sure she owed a debt to him.

The memory of all I learned has remained always. He would paint lots and lots of little pictures, quite often only 6 x 3in and he would say, 'Nellie Bly if ever you should want to paint, start with little pictures.' Those little pictures left a deep impression on me.

And indeed it was with small pictures she began.

Great-Uncle Charles inspired both of the elder Layfield children to draw and paint on a winter's evening. There were the usual hand-painted Christmas cards for Grandmother and the Aunts but Helen also produced a little book entitled 'Our House' to entertain her brothers and sisters. It was all about life in an imaginary tree-house they were supposed to have built.

If the young Helen ever cherished any ideas of being an artist, her father soon squashed them. 'Father said there were to be no more artists and painting,' she recalled. 'Thinking of pictures was forbidden. I must become a decent pianist. He loved the viola and violin and we had our own quartet which met every Sunday at home. I being the pianist in the piano quintet – I loved it. The music made picture and colour for me.'

In 1908 after the birth of Dorothy, the Layfield family moved from Lees High Street to an area called Clarkesfield, closer to Oldham. Their new house in Grasmere Road had the advantage of being next to a school which made it easier for Helen and George to get there rather than relying on Aunt Mary to take them. Gone were the carefree days when Helen could wander across to her grandmother's and be the indulged granddaughter. It was a short walk back up the hill to visit Grandmother and the Aunts, so contact was not broken and Helen's knowledge of local characters and happenings in Lees High Street continued unabated.

Events that happened in the High Street were a source of great interest and colour to all the folk in Lees and Oldham, and made a profound impression on the young Helen. There were occasions like the Whit Walks when the mills and shops closed. Everyone made an effort to dress up, indeed it was one of the few times in the year when some people purchased new clothes. That provided good business for Shaw's the tailors, but many of the locals bought their white clothes on the market stalls in Oldham. The Whit Walks took place on a Friday and this was a public holiday when the members of the different Sunday Schools, Anglican, Catholic, Church and Chapel, paraded through the street with their banners. For Helen it was a splendid sight but one which she could only observe and not be part of the procession as she would have loved. Although her mother's family, the Shaws, were churchgoers, her father would have no truck with religion and made sure none of his children attended church for more than the obligatory weddings and funerals.

Funerals could provide elaborate parades if the deceased had been a person of substance, and Helen painted several such scenes with glossy black horses and mourners in their best clothes. But the delight of these pictures is often in the homely details – the concern over food to be served afterwards, the child with a catapult or others taking the opportunity to settle a dispute whilst no one is looking.

Although visits of royalty to this part of the world were a rarity, they were certainly memorable and sent the young Helen, the Aunts and most of the inhabitants of Oldham into a state of great excitement. It was the processions naturally which stuck in her mind and offered great scope for pictures. Such an event would also enable her to enjoy a flight of fantasy, developing the idea that Queen Alexandra might call in at Grandmother's for a cup of tea and to exchange helpful cookery tips.

It was not surprising, given the time, the place, and Helen's independent spirit, that she should have painted the suffragettes' march. From 1905 the women's suffrage question was coming to the fore and nowhere more so than in Oldham. Annie Kenny, a mill girl from

Suffragette march through Oldham   Courtesy Oldham Library

Lees, was an active campaigner alongside Christabel Pankhurst from Manchester. This captured Helen's imagination and was to inspire several paintings. Whether Helen's mother and the Aunts were really sympathetic to the suffragettes' cause is not known but Helen evidently thought they would be and she was equally sure her father would not be, justifiably, it seems, in view of his unstinting disregard for her talent or her hopes.

As well as the reality of street pageants in Helen's childhood, there was the delightful fictional world created by Great-Aunt Jane. She lived higher up the hill from Lees at Springhead and was routinely visited on a Tuesday afternoon. Helen had vivid memories of the dark Victorian interior of her house:

Her rooms were dark and gloomy. Her curtains were dark-red plush with bobbles down the edge; her tables were covered in plush and so was the mantelpiece. Her walls were very dark and covered with pictures; many of them were of battles, of castles being stormed and men and horses being shot and lying dead. I did not like them.

But the attraction was Great-Aunt Jane's story-telling. She related a homespun version of God and Old Testament events which were firmly rooted in the locality. These Helen elaborated further in her art, and turned up years later in a sequence of pictures, and a book, she called *'In the beginning,' said Great-Aunt Jane.* The delight of these pictures lies in the way in which Helen was able to weave together various strands from her family, the Bible and the Oldham scenery into surreal images and stories: tales of Jacob's ladder or a God, with braces and a spotted handkerchief, who sits on the roof lamenting the way humans treat the world, or Jonah's whale, with big tears in his eyes, appearing at the landing stage of the lake in the Alexandra Park, a place well known to all the inhabitants of Oldham.

The lake in Alexandra Park, Oldham   Courtesy Oldham Library

Although Helen was later to say she never went to school and took lessons at the kitchen table, she actually attended school until the age of fourteen. As she was about to leave, the headmaster of Clarkesfield Council School suggested Helen might try for a John Platt scholarship to Oldham Art School. That did not go down well with her father who thought his daughter would be better learning some housewifely skills from her mother and if she needed a hobby, he would rather it was musical. Helen won the battle and in the late summer of 1914 had been awarded the necessary scholarship to begin a full-time course at Oldham School of Art. However, she said ruefully, 'I'm afraid being let loose at the age of fourteen did not keep me at my studies. I had the time of my life.'

Helen's father once again laid down the law, concerning what she might and might not study at the art school. Because he had no time for anything arty, he insisted she study craft subjects that might be useful and did not involve an unhealthy interest in the human body. As a result Helen studied jewellery design, which suited her natural aptitude for making things. There was also some opportunity to

work on stained glass and needlework designs, as well as clay modelling. But a chance to draw and paint presented itself on the occasional Saturday sketching trips the art school arranged in the Cheshire countryside.

Helen's full-time art schooling lasted for around two years during which her father grumbled incessantly that it was a waste of time. Then he declared that enough was enough and 'the tomfoolery had to stop'. The impact of the First World War presented him with a reason. His workforce had been conscripted and if the business was going to continue then his daughter must work.

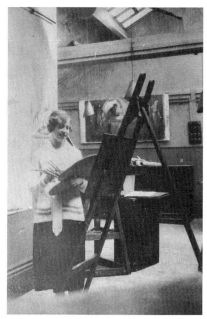

Helen at art school in Oldham

Freddie Layfield traded as a supplier of hardware and smallware (a term used to cover all manner of goods, from haberdashery through to gas mantles, writing-paper, polishes and, of course, Budnip's Patent Powders) to the many small shops operating in every street from someone's front room. Layfield senior had set him up in business with a large warehouse and two men to drive the horses and 'vans' that delivered the goods.

When Helen found herself pressed into service she was kitted out in a tweed coat, long skirt and a man's shirt and remembers being told to 'look grown-up', which must have been difficult for someone barely five-foot tall. Initially she walked from shop to shop with a small attaché case full of samples and an order book, but later she was permitted to drive Gertie, the pony, and the trap and go further afield collecting and delivering orders. Once again, her experiences were stored to be translated later into pictures.

Although her full-time art schooling was over, Helen carried on with evening classes for a further three years, gaining a City & Guilds in jewellery design, studying embroidery and finding out more about the rudiments of drawing and painting. These evenings could hold unexpected dramas. The Germans sent Zeppelins over to bomb Bolton on one of the nights Helen was returning from her evening class. Her family were terrified she might have been caught up in the attack and were hugely relieved when she walked in through the door. That incident and several others from the war years provided her with topics to paint later. For example, she depicted a battalion of soldiers marching through Oldham to go to war, local horses being taken to the railway station for transport to the front, and even a scene of fire-fighters trying to put out the fire in a row of cottages in Seven Sisters Road in London, bombed during this war.

When the First World War was over, she continued working in her father's business until around 1920, but increasingly this became part-time. As a girl, she was expected to spend more time helping her mother in the home in preparation for marriage. By 1920 her place in the business had been taken by her brother George who was permitted to drive father's car, a task solely reserved for men.

Adventures with the car, purchased in 1916, provided Helen with another source of material for paintings. These pictures are some of the few that include her father because as the driver, she said, he could not be left out. But Father, with so little time or regard for her art and his insistence that it was a male world, finds no real home in Helen Bradley's world.

It was at the art school that Helen encountered Tom Bradley, a tall, brooding young man regarded by many as the star pupil. He concentrated fully on his vocation and paid little attention to the giggly girl students. During the First World War he was sent to the trenches with the Lancashire Fusiliers where he suffered so badly from a gas attack that he was given up for dead. Eventually he recovered sufficiently to make his way home to Oldham, to the shock of his family who had received official notification that he had been 'killed in action'.

After the war there was some discussion about whether Tom might go to study at the Slade School in London, as the principal of Oldham Art School recommended. However Tom's father thought it more prudent for his son to go into commercial art so he took a job as a designer in the textile trade.

It was around 1922 that Tom and Helen met up again, this time at the local golf club which Helen had joined and where most of Tom's family were active members. Tall, silent Tom and tiny, vivacious Helen became engaged but did not marry for several years.

Unsettled by his war experiences, Tom gave up his design work and took a job as a travelling salesman for a company making fish and chip ranges. Not only did it suit his temperament at the time but it paid well enough for him to save towards their marriage.

The two were married in November 1926 when Helen was twenty-six and Tom twenty-seven, on a day when the fog was so thick many guests could not find the church, causing the ceremony to be delayed.

The newly-weds went to live in a pleasant suburb of Oldham, further away from the busy High Street in Lees where she had spent her early years. Now Helen turned her artistic talents to creating home furnishings and expertly tailored clothes for them both. She also found she had to take care of Tom on occasions when he suffered several frightening bronchial attacks resulting from the damage to his lungs from gas attacks in the trenches.

The newly-weds, 1926

It was accepted that Tom was the only artist in the family and he resumed his work as a designer, this time for a firm in Manchester who specialised in hand-printed fabrics and retained the services of Vanessa Bell and Duncan Grant on their books to produce the occasional design. One of the high spots in Tom's design career was the creation of fabrics for the renowned ocean liner, the *Queen Mary*, in 1934.

When Helen had two children, Peter in 1927 and Betty in 1931, she found herself fully occupied looking after them and making all their clothes right down to their shoes. It was not that money was short, but Helen, who loved to make things, purchased a cobbler's last and learned the art of shoe-making.

The Second World War caused an upheaval in the Bradley family as it did for so many. Tom's job ended when his company was closed down under Emergency Regulations so he took on freelance work. Helen leased a knitting-wool shop which provided an outlet for her creative energy as she also knitted garments to sell, by hand and on her knitting machine.

After the Second World War, Tom resumed his textile design working on a freelance basis. One of his principal clients, the John Lewis Partnership, was in London and Manchester which involved a lot of commuting so it made sense for the Bradleys to move south to Stanmore in Middlesex in 1945. There Helen joined an art club in Harrow Weald and took up painting again as a hobby. When the children were at school, she made good use of the proximity to the London art galleries; these visits, far more than her efforts at the art club, shaped the art of Helen Bradley.

During her visits to the National Gallery, Helen became fascinated by the winter landscapes of Hendrick Avercamp (1585–1634). His paintings teemed with figures engaged in their own activities and Helen found herself studying these pictures for ages. Some people have suggested Helen Bradley's art owes much to that of LS Lowry, without considering the possible influence Avercamp had on her. Certainly one of her early works is inscribed 'After Avercamp' and admits to his influence (see page 23).

Helen Bradley's inspiration came from several sources. Other gallery excursions took her to the British Museum where she became captivated by the work of Mughal artists of the sixteenth and seventeenth centuries, whose paintings served as an illustrated diary of court life. 'The real influence on me is early Mughal art painters,' she once said. 'They are simple and they all have a story, the story of Krishna and Radha. I have a story too, my family.' When she looked to her family as a subject, Helen found it essential to narrate their story, not just as a picture on paper or canvas, but with a separate paragraph pasted on the back.

There were many other features Helen admired in Mughal art which she was to adapt for her use. She noticed the figures appeared flat and without perspective or shadow. In portraits faces were often shown in profile with large eyes. At the same time there was a painstaking attention to detail and realism. The patterns and ornamentation in the little Mughal pictures come out in Helen's work in her delineation of brickwork or stone in street scenes, or the meticulous way she paints interiors.

Other Mughal paintings have a bustle of activity that has been frozen mid-action, with the spectator looking from above; Helen said it was 'as though they were perched on a cloud looking down'. She found this viewpoint especially useful when painting large, busy street scenes, like the procession on page 41. The Oriental artists used bright jewel-like colours which Helen adored, so she restricted her palette to five colours.

During her time in London, Helen also attended the art school in Harrow for a short time, but once again felt she was wasting her time. She gained far more from looking, thinking and absorbing ideas from works in public collections. Some Chinese watercolour artists caught her eye. Helen thought their work exquisite and read more in an effort to learn how their effect was achieved. It had been the practice of one artist to leave his paper outside overnight to let the dew soak it through before he started work. When Helen started painting, her homely version of this treatment was to soak the paper in the bath overnight then drain it off in the morning. The Chinese artist whose landscapes she admired most was Tao-chi (1630–1707), a Buddhist monk from the Ming family. He used very long brush strokes to draw mountains and valleys and then short precise brush strokes to serve as men, houses and distant trees. Reading avidly about his technique, Helen discovered that he set out to find beauty in unattractive surroundings and wanted to show the positive side of life through his art. One of the most helpful things she read was a saying attributed to him: 'Where do I belong, to what school? I belong to myself, I use my own manner of painting.'

Years later when asked about the artistic influences in her life, Helen recalled some pictures seen:

…when my children were starting school and I used to go to meet them. On the way I passed a house of an old friend of both my father and in-laws. He was a delightful old gentleman who had collected throughout his life the little pictures of the Norwich School. I believe he had a small Constable or two. There were 500 or more in the sitting room. The walls were covered and they overflowed on to the little tables and his writing desk. One was his favourite and it was no bigger than 5 x 3½in. It was of a cold wet rainy day. 'Just look at that rain,' he would say, 'It is really wet, and windy and desolate, isn't it? Look at those poor wet cows sheltering. That is what I call a picture. And look at this. It's almost dark and the moon is just coming up. Look at that mist rising

over that marshy land.' You could look and look at it and almost smell the salty peat marshes… The memory of that room will always remain and what an influence it has been.

Helen's time in the south of England provided her with many ideas with which she began experimenting. In 1952 Tom Bradley decided to retire from textile design and paint portraits and flowers to commission, so they moved to Mobberley and then in 1958 to Wilmslow in Cheshire. Helen joined the art school in Stockport for a while but once again felt she was getting nowhere until she joined classes at the Wilmslow Guild. Here she found sympathy and help in the search for her style. Her husband Tom remembered that 'she painted some rather good impressionistic landscapes and a few studies of buildings which were quite imaginative, she painted creatively.' Under the direction of her tutor, Helen tried painting in the style of a number of artists such as Picasso, Graham Sutherland and John Piper. 'I remember that she sold these, I forget how many of them, for around £1 each,' Tom added. 'Day comes as a glowing furnace' is an early Bradley work. She had tried drawing figures before as the pastel picture 'Two Sisters in Ireland' dated 1953 demonstrates, but she never felt happy with her work. Interestingly, this early picture has a story pasted to the back. Helen had discovered that she could not paint pictures with people in without feeling the need to tell the viewer something of the characters in the picture.

In 1964 the Bradleys bought May Cottage in Cartmel and moved to the edge of the Lake District. Helen later recalled:

Everyone seemed to be painting here, and the countryside is very beautiful…For years and years I have said to myself, isn't that lovely. I'd love to paint it. All sorts of odd things from flower in pots to sunlit cottages, a tree turning into a golden wonder, but the fleeting joys passed and I did nothing about it. But when I suddenly decided to paint, I did begin suddenly. I had been a walk by myself, and looking back towards the fell I saw a picture. Dark sky and a bare sunlit tree looking a lovely warm pinky brown. I said, 'I'll paint that, I'll paint it small and I'll paint one little picture every day then when I've got 365 that will be a record of our days.'

The idea was there, but there was still the problem of art materials. Tom had his paints and brushes which Helen would not dream of helping herself to; after all he was the professional and she the amateur. Instead she said:

I had to buy hardboard, cut it up and give it a grounding, which I did with white emulsion paint. I bought black, white, yellow ochre, Winsor blue and light red, and a small palette knife and a brush.

This was the early 1960s and Helen Bradley the artist had begun work.

Her early landscapes put Great-Uncle Charles's advice to her all those years ago into practice: 'Nellie Bly, if ever you should want to paint, start with little pictures.' She began working with oils, employing unconventional tools to apply and remove the paint. Kitchen implements like old fish slices, bread knives, even household nails, were used to scrape at the paint which Helen applied as thickly as possible. Although she admits to buying a brush, she did not use it much, preferring her hands or fingernails for spreading the paint. On other occasions she filched worn-out brushes from the rubbish her husband threw away.

As Tom collected his things and went off to the studio at Ashtree Cottage, which he rented, to work on his commissions, Helen quietly assembled her pieces. Some days she caught buses to take her round the Lake District sketching. Then on other days she would remain at home and work on her landscapes.

She also experimented with watercolours during the 1960s, interpreting what she had seen and read about the technique employed by Chinese artists. In the large trees and water scene on page 24, Helen worked hard to achieve the misty, dreamy effects these artists created on wet paper. The misty trees watercolour on page 28 is dated 1966.

When Tom announced he was joining the local Saddleworth Art Group, Helen decided she would too, as much for the social life as anything she said. Although she certainly did her fair share of making tea and providing cakes, Helen went sketching with the group but never exhibited any paintings. She recalled it was at one of the group's exhibitions held at the Museum at Uppermill, Saddleworth, that she met the artist L S Lowry and told him of the difficulties she was experiencing trying to paint figures. 'Paint someone you know well,' he is alleged to have told her. 'Go home and paint your mother.' This, she said, was the turning-point. No longer hampered by what she should and should not do when it came to portrait work, Helen painted her mother resplendent in her fine silks and splendid hat, as she remembered her.

That was the spur she needed.

Away I went, painting the people I have loved; the horses, dogs and cats which were part of our lives, with an ease which has completely astonished me. I would like to say thank you to LS Lowry for the gentle proddings he has given me, for without him I should never have had the courage to begin such a stupendous task.

Her husband said that she never took her pictures seriously at the time because they were purely imaginative portrayals of episodes she remembered in her childhood.

After Mother came the rest of the now familiar cast and with them came the stories. Helen said she began this subject because she wanted to show her grandchildren what life had been like in Edwardian times. She said:

I am painting a leisurely age, an age of hansom cabs and growlers of trains which waited at stations while we sorted out our heavy trunks and leather Gladstone bags. There was time to walk up and down the platform chatting to friends and then we would steam out with dignity into the countryside.

Helen's daughter, Betty, remembers the excitement when Helen found her feet.

Once she got on to her figures there was no stopping her. She was quite unscrupulous and so determined that no one would stand in her way. She'd found something that was herself. In the past she had never been so determined; she always gave in to her husband and her children, it was always what they wanted. She didn't seem to have an opinion of her own, she never said what she wanted.

The early 1960s were years of frenetic activity. Once Tom had gone off of a morning or late at night after he was asleep, Helen worked away at her pictures. The results were stuffed under the bed and may well have stayed there, signed with a little fly in the corner, had there not been a thunderstorm.

One summer's day in 1965 during a torrential downpour, a couple of women took shelter under Helen's front porch. Ever hospitable, Helen invited them in for a cup of tea to wait for the storm to pass. In the course of conversation she told them of her paintings and even fetched some examples from under the bed. They departed and

Helen forgot about the episode. Shortly afterwards she received a letter from the small museum and art gallery in Uppermill, near Lees, offering her a one-woman exhibition.

Helen was astounded. She had never shown any of her paintings in public before and most were not even framed. Not liking to spend too much money on a venture that she thought stood little chance of success, Helen bought materials and Tom set about making the frames. The small landscapes were easy but the childhood pictures, being larger, presented more problems. When she discovered knots or marks in the wood she had bought for framing, rather than throw those pieces on the fire, she took her brush out and continued the scene out across the mounting and on to the frame, creating the most amazing effects. Unconventional that might have been, but Helen never expected anyone to want her childhood pictures, so although they were exhibited they were never priced.

On 17 November 1965 the first one-woman exhibition of Helen Layfield's work opened. Concerned about the impact of her pictures on Tom's work as a local portrait painter, she used her maiden name. Her pictures had a little fly in the corner but no name on them. As the catalogue shows, Helen's work was in transition. The first 14 works listed are instantly recognisable as the famous childhood pictures, but what follows is an equal number of 'little pictures', those small landscapes in oils inspired by Great-Uncle Charles. The remainder of the pictures in her first exhibition were also experimental. The 'Flowers' were evidently inspired by Tom Bradley's delicate flower paintings. There are watercolour landscapes demonstrating the Chinese influence, and others with intriguing titles like 'Rather Like Lowry' and one she calls 'Lord why hast thou forsaken me'. In the place where the price would go she has put, 'don't think anyone would like this.'

There was local interest in this exhibition and amongst those who came was Lord Rhodes of Saddleworth. 'I remember he sat in that little museum on a shooting stick all that Sunday afternoon,' she recalled. To her surprise it was the paintings of her family that he sat gazing at in admiration. He advised her to 'forget all the other stuff' and gave Helen the address of a London gallery he was certain would be interested in her work. Tom took some photographs and sent them off, not really expecting to hear anything.

The response was better than they dared hope. The Mercury Gallery, in Cork Street, was about to put on an exhibition of naïve painters and requested six of her family pictures immediately. These were sent, and sold out as soon as the exhibition opened in December 1966. This prompted the Mercury Gallery to give her a one-woman show of her own in 1970. She chose to show some of her family paintings alongside some of her landscapes which she considered 'proper' pictures. The childhood pictures sold instantly, the landscapes came back. That determined the future of Helen Bradley's painting.

In 1971 she had another one-woman exhibition and all the paintings were based on her childhood memories. Once again the public could not get enough of Helen Bradley's work; she was famous and fêted by the media, with reporters from magazines, radio and television falling over each other to get an interview with the 'famous pensioner' as they liked to dub her.

At the 1971 exhibition her paintings were seen by the Managing Director of the publishers Jonathan Cape, Tom Maschler, who instantly knew these scenes would make a superb children's book. He chose 26 pictures from the exhibition, complete with their stories pasted on the backs, and wove them into the very successful *And Miss Carter Wore Pink: scenes from an Edwardian Childhood*. This first book, published in 1971, took its title from one of the characters who appeared in many of the pictures and ensured Miss Carter would feature in almost all the pictures which followed.

Invitations for Helen to exhibit came flooding in after that and at such a rate Helen could barely keep up; nevertheless she managed to stage an exhibition almost every two years, as well as supply the insatiable demand for private commissions. Visitors turned up on her doorstep at the little cottage in Cartmel and, despite being fully occupied painting, Helen always stopped, invited them in and gave them tea. It meant that she was often painting far into the night to make up the time she had spent baking cakes in the morning in case anyone called, and entertaining those who did call in the afternoon. To her immense delight, and pride, two of her paintings, entitled 'The End of a Gradeley Day' and 'Goodbye Punch and Judy', hung in the Royal Academy in 1973. As her fame grew, so did requests for images from her work to appear on merchandise from place mats to tee-shirts to jigsaw puzzles. However, she resisted the financial inducements, preferring to stay true to herself as an artist. To the surprise of someone so quintessentially English, Helen found her work in demand abroad as well. Even as early as 1967 her paintings were requested for exhibition in Los Angeles and her success led to an American following and even the formation of a Miss Carter Club.

There has also been a great following for Helen Bradley's paintings in Japan and, although Helen did not live to see it, there was a major exhibition of her work in Osaka in Japan, in 1993.

By the mid-1970s Helen Bradley was famous, earning large sums from her paintings and constantly in demand for interviews or as a guest at art exhibitions. Remembering the struggle most artists go through to gain recognition, Helen gave freely of her time and money to support young artists setting out. Many a local artist has reason to be grateful to Helen Bradley for her kind words of encouragement and the purchase of one of their works. But as a woman now well into her seventies, Helen found the pressure of fame, and the business side of art, a great burden. Tom, who had initially been sceptical of her talent, supported her as much as he could with advice and practical help, but his eyesight deteriorated in the early 1970s and he went blind.

It was in 1971 that Helen and Tom were fortunate enough to be introduced to Keith Lee by the Lancashire watercolour artist and cabinet maker, William Brown. Keith was working as a freelance manufacturer's agent, distributing limited edition prints of L S Lowry's work from offices in Princess Street, Manchester. As Tom and Helen were finding themselves inundated with requests for prints and exhibitions of Helen's work, Tom suggested to Keith they form a partner-

Tom and Helen, early 1970s

ship to handle this side of the business professionally and ensure the integrity of Helen Bradley's work was maintained. On 20 April 1972, Miss Carter Publications was born in Manchester and relocated to 25 Silverwell Street, Bolton in 1976, where it remains today. Miss Carter Publications soon found their high quality signed limited edition prints of Helen Bradley's paintings were eagerly sought by collectors. Tom enjoyed his involvement in the company and regularly visited the offices in Manchester, and later Bolton, up until his retirement in 1983, when he was succeeded in the company by Patricia Lee. Miss Carter Publications has continued publishing high quality editions of some of Helen's paintings ever since and celebrated its thirtieth anniversary in 2002.

Helen took an interest in Miss Carter Publications but creating new paintings was her first love.

By 1978 she was seventy-eight, and still working hard at her painting. The following year she received a letter to say she had been awarded the MBE in the Queen's Honours List; this was the greatest honour Helen could imagine. Shortly before she was due to attend the Palace in June 1979, she had a heart attack and went into hospital. After a few days she returned home against the doctor's advice.

Friends and family called to see her a day or so later and, although not at all well, Helen made a supreme effort to get up and sit by the fire to receive them. After they had gone, Tom got her into bed as she was exhausted. Helen Bradley died in her sleep on Wednesday 18 July 1979. The MBE she so richly deserved arrived by post. Helen Bradley had painted such wonderfully imaginative accounts of the Queen coming to tea when she was a child, but was ultimately denied the honour of meeting the real Queen.

Helen's fame has continued unabated since her death, with her paintings in even greater demand than they were in her lifetime. Pictures of her childhood stories can change hands for substantial five-figure sums, which Helen would have found incredible. Sadly, Helen did not live to see the staging of the ballet production of her famous childhood stories. This was the only alternative use of her work she had permitted and she even donated two of her paintings to be auctioned to help with the cost of the production. In 1980 the Northern Ballet premiered 'Miss Carter Wore Pink' at the Sadler's Wells Theatre in the presence of Princess Margaret, an event Helen would have delighted in. Nevertheless, exhibitions of Helen Bradley's paintings, showing a view of life at the beginning of the twentieth century, continue to please the public in the twenty-first century.

Helen Bradley Copyright Geoffrey Shryhane

The Main Cast in Helen Bradley's Pictorial World

Miss Carter (who wore Pink) lives with her maid, 'young Sarah', near the Aunts. Her parents and brother have died leaving her with 'private means'. She has set her sights on Mr Taylor, the widowed bank manager, and is trying to manoeuvre him into a proposal of marriage. Everyone is in awe of Miss Carter because she dresses in the latest fashions, created for her in Manchester. Her passion for pink in all its shades even extends to the wallpaper in her house.

Aunt Charlotte is a pretty blonde eighteen-year-old who smells of April violets and lives with her mother and sisters opposite Helen. She has caught the eye of the new young curate, Reverend Albert Green.

Aunt Edith is Father's youngest sister who lives with Grandfather Layfield in Blackpool. She regularly weeps over unrequited love.

Aunt Frances is small and dark haired and has a long-running romance with James Alfred, the chemist, whom she will ultimately marry. Aunt Frances teaches at Leesfield Church Sunday School and lives with her mother and sisters.

Aunt Mary is described as 'the more sturdy' of the sisters and needs to be since it falls to her to supervise most of the household tasks and weave cloth on the loom at the top of the house when she has time. If that were not enough, Aunt Mary goes over the road to help with washing and cooking at Helen's home.

Grandmother Shaw is often painted along with the Aunts but takes a passive role in the stories.

George is Helen's young brother and playmate. Together they appear in most pictures dressed in sailor suits. George is usually aged around three or four and gets bullied by the naughty Willie Murgatroyd.

The pets, Gyp and Barney, are two dogs with curly tails seen in most pictures. The cats Martha and Nelson also feature but George's marmalade cat is mentioned but never seen.

Great-Aunt Jane is married to Uncle Tom and they live with their maid Martha. The children do not enjoy visiting her because she is tall, thin and forbidding. Pictures on her walls are just as grim, showing war scenes littered with dead and dying horses. Great-Aunt Jane's saving grace is that she can tell wonderful stories and is the narrator of the enchanting series entitled 'And in the Beginning … said Great-Aunt Jane'.

The Murgatroyds are a rough lot who live in the street behind Helen. They turn up regularly because Mrs Murgatroyd cleans for Helen's mother and bring her children Willie and Annie twice a week to share George and Helen's lessons at the kitchen table. Willie is the naughty boy in Helen's stories who bullies them with peashooter, fists and ink pellets.

Mrs Maitland and Emily live next door to Miss Carter, and are regular visitors to the Aunts although Mrs Maitland is not popular. She has been a widow for five years and tries everyone's patience to the limit by becoming weepy or 'feeling a little ill' when she wants attention. Everyone feels sorry for Emily, a sweet patient girl, who has a lot to put up with. Mr Taylor is paying a great deal of interest to Emily, which makes Miss Carter jealous. Ultimately Emily will be the one who becomes the second Mrs Taylor.

Mr Taylor, the bank manager, is a regular visitor to the Aunts which sends all the ladies into a flutter. John Joseph Taylor, whose wife Hilda died over a year ago, is no longer in deep mourning. Local unattached ladies think he must be looking for a second wife now and there are no shortage of volunteers because he dresses well and has an alluring masculine smell of cigars and pomade. His every move is watched and analysed as he seems to waver between Miss Carter and Emily Maitland. Eventually he will choose Emily.

Mrs Hope-Ainsworth, Nellie and Bertie live further up the hill and are better off than the Aunts. The family are pretentious and so not considered part of the close circle of friends. That doesn't stop them turning up, which is a nuisance since Nellie is a dreadful girl who eavesdrops conversations then tells tales.

Great-Aunt Buckley and her maid Polly live at Greengate Street in Glodwick, closer to Oldham. The children do not enjoy visiting her dark old house and she does not welcome children either. The only attraction is Snippets, the biggest black cat you ever did see, who will obligingly chase after feathers tied to string.

Reverend Albert Green, the new curate at Leesfield, is fast becoming a regular visitor to Grandmother's house now that he has fallen in love with Aunt Charlotte.

Annie Simpson used to clean for Helen's mother, Miss Carter, and the vicar. She was a cheerful, hard-working woman who sang Salvation Army hymns lustily as she worked. When she died having her fourth baby, Mrs Murgatroyd took over the cleaning.

James Alfred, the chemist, lives with his mother. He promised his father on his death-bed never to marry, but to stay at home and look after mother. This has meant that when he fell in love with Aunt Frances, it would be a protracted romance. His mother will finally consent to the wedding when James is sixty.

Biddy Murphy, an elderly Irish woman with numerous children, lives close to the Murgatroyds. She loves children and will tell them yarns about leprechauns as she doles out home-made bread. She also tells far more scary stories involving a tiger who lives down a local alleyway and can be heard roaring.

Grandfather Layfield at Blackpool is a great favourite with Helen and George. They love to go to his house for the holidays and he will collect them from the station in the trap pulled by Prince.

Uncle John and Aunt Josephine live in Manchester with their three children. Uncle John is a brother of Helen's father but they frequently argue.

Aunt Annie is the younger sister of Helen's father. She marries Willie Sugden in 1910 and they move to the Isle of Man but there is high drama when she leaves her husband after a month and runs away to London. She says she cannot live with a man who insists she give up educating herself to concentrate on him.

Great-Uncle Charles is the famous artist who spends his time between London and Paris. His visits to Lees bring a whiff of excitement.

Florrie Samuel is an elderly friend of Grandmother's but she is a fearful gossip so everyone goes quiet when she turns up.

Mary Ellen, another of Grandmother's friends, is married to John Henry but dies leaving him with four unmarried daughters.

Alice Ann Bailey lives with her mother next door to Grandmother and the Aunts. She is aged forty and a great friend of Aunt Mary's. Although she comes from a middle-class family, she shocks everyone by marrying Jim Wilson, a widower with four sons, who is a mill worker, rather than remain a spinster.

Afternoon on Ice

This early painting by Helen Bradley is inscribed 'After Avercamp' on the back. It shows the influence this seventeenth century Dutch artist had on her work

The Mountains and Trees

On the back Helen has written: The mountain and trees float on the waters of a lake and light comes down from Heaven. From the song of never-ending grief from the T'ang Dynasty.

watercolour   Signed Helen Layfield Bradley 1964

24

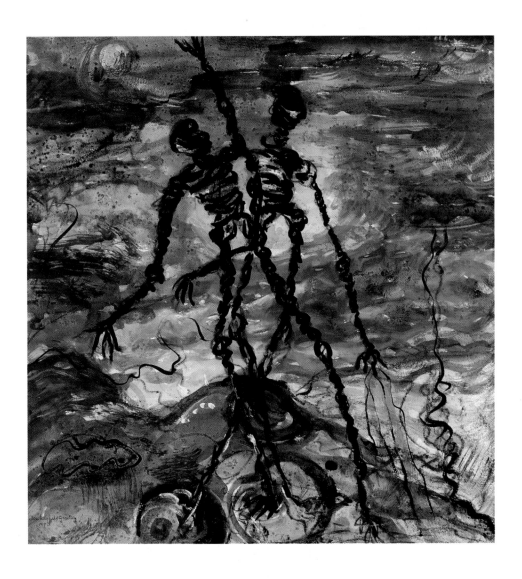

The Day Comes Glowing Like a Furnace

The day comes, glowing like a furnace, all the arrogant and the evil-doers shall be chaff, and that day when it comes shall set them ablaze, says the Lord, it shall leave them neither root nor branch… and that day I have painted after the manner of Graham Sutherland from the last verse in the Old Testament.

mixed media   Signed Helen Layfield Bradley 1953

Wistfully the Young Sister Looked Beyond Her Garden

Wistfully the young sister looked beyond her garden, out to the fields and the distant blue hill, out into a world she would never know – 'For you cannot go, you must stay with me and guard our home,' said the old sister. 'Home,' sighed the young one, 'Out there are cities and perhaps love,' and she sighed again and again for love, for love.

mixed media

Once Upon a Time There Lived Two Sisters

Once upon a time there lived two sisters in a lonely castle in Ireland. They were very poor, but very gentle; the youngest sister was very pretty and as well as being pretty she had a sweet and gentle nature. Adele, the eldest sister, refused the gentle Rose all suitors, saying she must remain with her to care for and guard their castle. Now, at last, Rose sees that her chance for freedom will soon be here, for the hand of death is very near for poor Adele.

mixed media Signed Helen Layfield Bradley 1953

Untitled

watercolour, 1969   Signed with a fly

'Go,' Said God!

'Go,' said God, 'thou art a seer – go out among my people and say unto them, 'the Wrath of God shall descend on all who obey me not! They shall be called sinners."

mixed media, 1953   Signed Helen Layfield Bradley

Winter Snow

This oil painting was Helen's first experiment with a large canvas. She was pleased with her efforts and hung the picture in her bedroom where it remained for the rest of her life.

All on an April Evening

It was on an April evening – Mother said, 'Let us go for a walk in the
Enchanted Garden, it is such a beautiful evening. Come along
children, it is too nice to go to bed,' so George and I helped Mother,
the Aunts and Miss Carter (who wore Pink) to gather daffodils to
take back to Grandma, who was feeling tired after the first day of our
holidays at Blackpool, and the year was 1908.

Caught in an April Shower

All on an April Evening. Mother, Father, George and I and the dogs
Gyp and Barney were coming home in the trap after a ride in the
spring countryside of Cheshire when we were caught in an April
shower, and the year was 1907.

'We Had Better Turn Back,' said Mother

'We had better turn back,' said mother, 'it's looking like rain.' Mother hadn't an umbrella and George and I hadn't our coats. We had Miss Carter (who wore Pink) and Mrs Maitland and Dear Emily with us, and when Mrs Maitland saw Mr Taylor (the Bank Manager) coming to escort us home, she was sure she had a cold coming on, but Mr Taylor held Dear Emily's hand and Miss Carter (who had on her new hat) looked cross. 'Dear me,' said Aunt Mary to Aunt Frances, 'now there'll be trouble, surely he can't be fancying Dear Emily,' and the year was 1908.

On Windy Days We Went to Lytham

On windy days we went to Lytham, where the weather wasn't quite as bad as walking along the prom or the sands at Blackpool. Grandpa would saddle Prince to the wagonette and away we went through the back lanes to Lytham. George and I always took our kites because the green was a good place to fly them, and afterwards we went into the town to see the shops and take home something nice for Grandma, and the year was 1907.

Isn't It Kind of Mr Taylor

'Oh Jane, isn't it kind of Mr Taylor to bring our shawls,' said Aunt Frances. 'Indeed it is,' said Mother, but Miss Carter (who wore Pink) took her pink shawl with a haughty 'Thank you' from Mr Taylor (the Bank Manager). It was a lovely April evening and everyone agreed we should go to the Enchanted Garden and see the wild cherry blossom and also gather bunches of wild daffodils to take back to Grandma. As we turned to walk home Aunt Charlotte whispered, 'Look he's taken her arm, perhaps he'll propose,' but he mustn't have done because she was stiff and huffy and, 'Oh dear,' said Mother, 'it's only our first walk of the holidays,' and we were at Blackpool in the year 1908.

Gathering Nuts in May

'Grandpa's waiting in the lane with Prince. I can hear him chewing his bit, and whatever Miss Carter (who wore Pink) and Mr Taylor (the Bank Manager) are dawdling along for, I don't know.' 'Well,' said Aunt Mary, 'We'd better wait. Oh Jane, wouldn't it be nice if he proposed to her,' so whilst we waited and called for them to hurry, George and I watched some little girls dance round an old dead tree. They held garlands of daisies and buttercups and they sang the funny old song, 'Here we come gathering nuts in May, nuts in May, nuts in May', and the year was 1906.

On a Warm Summer Afternoon we went to Daisy Nook

It was a very special place and was a great treat to go so far on a tramcar – then a walk through the fields and farms until we came to some real old-fashioned quaint cottages. There were trees and the River Irwell, clean and sparkling with ducks swimming about. One of the cottagers made home-made lemonade and we had tea, sitting on a form at a table spread with a white cloth. We had fresh home-baked bread and farm butter and blackberry jelly and the year was 1906.

One Warm Day

One warm afternoon Grandpa said, 'Would you all like to drive with me to Rawcliffe Hall, I want to see the farmer to ask his opinion about buying that pony 'Zober'. He thinks she's getting on a bit.' 'Oh Grandpa,' I cried, 'Think how happy Zober would be, if she came to live with us.' 'Well,' said Grandpa, 'Get your hats on, and we'll see what he says.' So Mother, the Aunts, also Miss Carter (who wore Pink) and Mr Taylor (the Bank Manager), and George and I were soon off in the wagonette with Prince, trotting along the lanes. Grandpa dropped us as soon as we entered the park. He always said that the walk through the quiet lane up to the farm would do us good, but Mother, Aunt Frances, Miss Carter and I didn't think so, because we didn't like cows and we didn't know when they would decide to come our way. Mr Taylor said that he would look after us, but for all that, we were always glad to see Grandpa and be safely behind Prince, and the year was 1907.

We Went for a Walk

We went for a walk to the park on May-day morning. It was a beautiful morning so Mother decided to call on Grandma and the Aunts and we would all walk to the park and on the way George and I would see all the horses dressed in their best hats and flowers in their harness. We saw a tiny May Queen with a piece of lace curtain for her veil, and Fanny (our strong-minded horse) looking very smart being driven along by Father who was taking Aunt Edith home, and the year was 1908.

Bell Horse Day in Lees

All the people in the village are out watching the horses go by. They are all trimmed with flowers or bells. Mother, Father, George and I and the three Aunts are waiting to see our horse, Fanny. In spite of her wearing her best hat she is behaving very badly, but Fanny is very strong minded and always insists on walking in front next to the Band. Father is going to help Ted lead her forward. Mr Taylor (the Bank Manager) goes to the aid of Miss Carter (who wore Pink) as she is afraid of Fanny, and the year was 1906 on a lovely May morning.

Whit Walks – Piccadilly Manchester

Father said, 'I want you all ready by the time I've brought the car round. We're all going to have lunch with Uncle John in his new bungalow. I will collect Miss Carter (who wore Pink) and Mr Taylor (the Bank Manager), then we'll be off.' We were soon ready and on our way to Manchester, but there was one thing we had all forgotten – that today was Whit Friday, so of course, when we got to Piccadilly we had to stop. The Whitsuntide Walk was just coming along. It was a most wonderful procession. There were bands and banners and everyone wore their new clothes. The procession went on and on and Father began to get very cross. We all thought of Uncle John wondering what had happened to us, and poor Aunt Josephine trying to keep our dinner warm, but it was no use, we had to wait and then slowly drive behind until we came to Kingsway, and the year was 1917

Whit Walks

King Edward VII Opened His First Parliament

Now we had a new King and a very happy young Queen, and all the people who had felt so sad and lost began to brighten up, especially when a new paper called *The Queen* could be purchased from the book stalls in Manchester, and it was there that Miss Carter (who wore Pink) found a copy and hurried back with it for everyone to look at. Then towards the end of February Great-Uncle Charles wrote asking the Aunts and Miss Carter to come to London and stay with him in his hotel. They would all go and see the State Opening of Parliament. Everyone would still be in mourning because it was only a few weeks since Queen Victoria's death, so they went and saw the King and Queen drive down the Mall. Our new Queen looked beautiful, they told Mother when they got back home. She wore a black dress trimmed with diamonds, and her hair was all little curls – how had she managed it? And they looked at one another – and wondered!

The Queen Who Came to Tea

The Great Day had arrived. Mother got us ready early and whilst waiting for Grandma and the Aunts, also Miss Carter (who wore pink) and Mr Taylor (the Bank Manager), Mother made a hamper of dainty sandwiches and little cakes. Father came round with our little wagonette with Fanny – even dear Fanny was wearing her best hat. We drove to Manchester to meet Uncle John, then father took Fanny back and left us with Uncle John, who took us along the route to see all the bunting and flags. People were filling the streets, the little girls in their white frocks and everyone in their best clothes, and down by the Cathedral there was the River Irwell with its steamer decorated with flags sailing up to Salford. The Police were beginning to clear the streets, so we went back along Long Millgate and saw the little Market. Then Uncle John drove us back and, it was time to take our places, we ate and enjoyed our sanwiches and the day was 13th July 1905.

The Queen Who Came to Tea

To George and me it was a very long wait, but gradually all sorts of thing came along the route. There were lots and lots of Policemen all towards Victoria Station. There were lots of Policemen left behind who walked up and down keeping people in order. Children marched along with their teachers and filled the stands in front of the Infirmary and in front of us. Then there was a commotion a long way down Market Street, and, at last, we could hear a jingle of horses. 'They're coming, they're coming, the Queen is coming', and now they came in sight. 'Oh, I can't see them,' I cried. 'Well, well', said Uncle John, 'come up on my shoulder,' and what a glorious view I had. the Police came first riding their beautiful horses. There were a great many of them and behind them we could see the Queen's Hussars and the four lovely greys and, 'oh it's the King and Queen, I can just see them'.

These two pictures originally made one complete frieze approximately 10'x3'.

The Queen of Sheba

'Well,' said Aunt Mary, 'the Queen of Sheba was very lovely. She wore a dress of green watered-silk and had lots of jewels and gold; but her palaces were poor places, with bad drains and plumbing. The Queen thought something had better be done. She heard about King Solomon and what a fine man he was, so she thought she'd better count out some gold and jewels to offer him in return for some help. One fine day she gathered together her camels, her men and her bags of treasure. She put her green watered-silk dress and her crown in a bag and set off. She came within sight of a beautiful place. 'My,' she said, 'it's just like Manchester Town Hall,' so she changed into her best dress, did her hair up with pins and put on her crown. Then she went to meet Solomon. He thought her lovely and she thought him handsome. With him was God, busy with rolls of plans, for being a great builder, God was helping Solomon with his drains.

We Gathered Dandelions in the Lanes

We gathered dandelions in the lanes behind Blackpool. Every summer Grandma made herb beer, so when the dandelions were at their best, Grandpa saddled Prince to the wagonette and Mother, George and I (and the dogs, Gyp and Barney), Grandma and the Aunts set out to gather baskets of blossoms. We also took Miss Carter (who wore Pink) and Aunt Edith, (Father's youngest sister), but now she was seventeen and was wearing her new black hat and having fallen in love with a boy called Harold, she sighed and murmured, 'Love, O Love, thou art as lovely as a Rose,' and the year was 1908.

One Summer's Day We Were Taken to the Park

One Summer's day we were taken in a hansom to the park to have our photographs taken. Mama wanted her profile taking – she said she looked the best that way. George – alas – would not open his eyes. Looking on were Miss Maitland and Miss Carter (who wore Pink) and the year was 1908.

The Park in Manchester

On Saturday afternoon, whilst staying with Uncle John and Aunt Josephine in Manchester, we always went for a walk to the park, because, as Uncle John said, the children could run about, the ladies could take turns in pushing Marion in her pram, and the gentlemen could talk to their hearts' content. How George and I loved it. I always begged to walk as far as the little gate so that I could look through to the beautiful houses and the quiet road where only smart carriages drawn by dainty horses went and there were nursemaids taking tiny tots for a walk. It was very quiet and peaceful and someday, I told George, I would go and live in one of those lovely houses and he could come and live in it with me, and the year was 1907.

This was a Special Treat (Picnic in a Cornfield)

This was a special treat for we had to drive with Fanny, our big horse, harnessed to the wagonette, through Manchester, along the Stockport Road as far as the open country beyond Slade Lane. There we had a beautiful picnic in a cornfield. George and I saw a Cheshire Lines train and our dogs, Gyp and Barney, met farm dogs and had lots to say to each other. As we jogged home behind Fanny and the sun went down, George and I fell asleep snuggled up to Grandma and the year was 1906.

Spring Lane

It was a lovely sunny afternoon as we all went for our afternoon walk along Spring Lane. There was Grandma, Mother, Aunt Mary, Aunt Frances, Aunt Charlotte, George and I with Gyp and Barney. We could see Miss Carter (who wore Pink) hurrying along upfront to meet Mr Taylor (the Bank Manager) but we had to stop because on the other side of the lane was Miss Winterbottom (who taught the infants). Grandma and Aunt Mary wondered where she was taking all her little ones while Aunt Frances and Aunt Charlotte went up to her. 'Oh Frances,' said Miss Winterbottom 'we're going haymaking. It will do the children good to be out of doors. Will you come and help us?' So Aunt Frances and Aunt Charlotte stayed behind to help Miss Winterbottom. 'Well,' said Mother, 'she'll need some help, there's Willie and Annie Murgatroyd going to join them and that dreadful boy's got his catapult with him.' George and I would have loved to have joined them but not with Willie Murgatroyd being there, and the year was 1907.

Aunt Edith was Seventeen and Wept for Love

Aunt Edith was seventeen and wept for love, and there on the sands at Blackpool she wanted to go home. 'I can't go any further,' she said, and tears ran down her pretty face. 'Oh dear,' said Mother, 'Whatever's the matter, do you feel ill dear.' 'No,' she said, 'I just want to go home.' So on that lovely afternoon we all turned back. 'I'll bet it's that boy she's been walking home with. I think he's gone off to College', and for the last few days of our holiday she moped. No more would she come and romp in Grandpa's hayfield, or make toffee in the kitchen. 'Well, never mind her,' said Aunt Mary. 'She's growing up.' Oh dear, it was sad, and the year was 1910.

Blackpool Sands

It was a warm sunny afternoon at Blackpool. The tide was going out leaving the sands firm and nice to walk on, so George and I asked Mother, Grandma and the Aunts, if we could all walk just past the Central Pier. We knew the Punch and Judy show would be there, and as soon as Punch saw us he would wave his little stick and say, 'I see you, you're here again,' which made everyone laugh. We also knew that Willie and Annie Murgatroyd would have built a big sandcastle, but, unfortunately we met Mrs Hope-Ainsworth with Bertie and Nellie, also Miss Carter (who wore Pink) and she was hurrying in front of Mr Taylor (the Bank Manager). Aunt Mary whispered to Mother that she was sure they'd quarrelled, and I did so hope they'd get engaged, and the year was 1907.

'Children,' Said Father and Mother

'Children,' said Father and Mother, 'You've had enough donkey rides for today, Tom wants to take them home, the tide is coming in quickly,' so George and I said goodbye to our favourite donkeys and joined Grandma, the Aunts, Miss Carter (who wore Pink) and Mr Taylor (the Bank Manager), who had just arrived to walk back with Miss Carter. But Mrs Hope-Ainsworth with Bertie and Nellie had joined us, and Mrs Hope-Ainsworth insisted on walking with Mr Taylor all the way home, which made Miss Carter very cross, and the year was 1906.

Blackpool

This is Real Blackpool Weather

'This is real Blackpool weather,' said Mr Taylor (the Bank Manager), 'come along ladies, a good walk along the sands will do us all good,' so Grandma, Mother, the three Aunts and Miss Carter (who wore Pink) tied on their veils, and away we all went. We met Willie and Annie Murgatroyd and Willie had his kite, so Mother let George and I run back for ours. The sea was rough and the kites sailed away nearly taking us with them. We met Mrs Hope-Ainsworth with Nellie and Bertie, and they walked along with us. When we got back to Grandpa's we all ate an enormous tea, and the year was 1907.

Blackpool Station

Grandpa was waiting for us on the platform at Waterloo Road Station. Mother hurried George and me, and the dogs (Gyp and Barney), and Miss Carter and Mr Taylor quickly up the steps and into Grandpa's wagonette, because Willie and Annie Murgatroyd came running after us. Grandpa stopped Willie, and told Annie to take him back to his mother. Annie said it didn't matter really, he'd only got the mumps and was very cross, and as we hurried along we could hear him screaming and roaring. We had to leave Father, Grandpa and the three Aunts to attend to our luggage and our two cats, Martha and Nelson, who had come with us.

Fred Walmsley's Concert Party

'Oh, the tide is in,' George and I had so looked forward to playing on the sands on our first day at Blackpool, but Mother said, 'Never mind, we'll go on the pier and see if Fred Walmsley's Pierrots are there,' and there they were just beginning their show with a new song – it was –

> In the year nineteen hundred and nine
> We shall all have a jolly fine time
> for the World, you see
> will belong to me
> in the year nineteen hundred and nine

How I glowed, how I felt something wonderful was going to happen, and in a haze of expectancy I ate one of Pye's Ices while Mother, the Aunts, and Grandma drank a cup of Sandow's Cocoa, and the year was 1908.

The Animals

God and the Animals

On Christmas Eve all the animals living around Lees and Belle Vue asked God to come down from his shed up Springfield where he was living. They wanted to tell him all their troubles. Here they are, all the animals I have known and loved, airing their views about humans, but our Tom being keen on music, taught them all to sing, and here he is standing on his box waiting for Leesfield Church to chime midnight. 'Then,' he said, 'You must be ready with your mouths open, and we'll all sing "Christians Awake, salute this happy Morn" for now it is Christmas Day,' and the year was 1906.

It Was A Happy Land

It was a Happy Land, Far, Far Away, sang Albert, the new Curate, and Miss Smith who urged the children from Mount Pleasant Mission to sing with all their might, but the children wanted to begin their treat straight away with the tea, and then the cakes and sweets. All the ladies from Leesfield had helped to make it a day to remember. Aunt Frances and Aunt Charlotte are seeing that everyone gets a mug of tea. Miss Carter (who wore Pink) came, but did not bring her apron, so she looked after our dogs, Gyp and Barney. Mother is also helping, but is rather anxious lest George and I go near the poor children especially one little boy who has put up his hand saying 'Please Miss, I feel sick.' 'Dear Me,' said Mother, 'what shall we do with him,' but we found out the poor little boy hadn't had anything to eat all day and had come over faint, and the year was 1907.

Grandma, The Aunts

Grandma, the Aunts, Mother, George and I, Miss Carter and, of course, the dogs, Gyp and Barney, had been to Great-Aunt Jane's birthday party. The day hadn't been as nice as our usual visits because we wore our best clothes and we had to sit still. We longed for her to tell us a story about God. She only had time to tell us a bit, but it was good news. 'Well,' she said, 'God has come to live in a shed not far from Harts Head Pike.' He had come to see what Lees, Oldham and Manchester were like but he was finding it rather cold and damp. Great-Aunt Jane hadn't seen him but she'd heard that Mrs Winterbottom was going to help him, and all the lost dogs had heard about his coming and had gone to live with him. How glad George and I were to know that God had come to live near us – we should not be afraid again of the Thing that lived on the moors. As we walked down to Lees we looked at God's shed and saw a light come on. God was home.

'In the Beginning,' Said Great-Aunt Jane

'In the beginning,' said Great-Aunt Jane, 'God was young and lived in foreign parts called "the Void". The Void was very dark, just like blue velvet. God lived in a shed but he wasn't happy because it was so dark. "I am living always at Night," he said. "I want Day." So he made a mixture in an old barrel, rolled it into balls and lit them with his matches. They gave out a beautiful white light. "Why," he said, "I'll call you Stars." But still they didn't give him Day. So he made a very big star with a bright yellow face which he polished with Brasso until it shone. Then he threw it from the highest point in the Void. It disappeared but soon it peeped over the rim and its light and warmth delighted him. "You are great and shall be called Sun." He laughed and was well pleased. That is enough now,' said Great-Aunt Jane, 'it is time for you to go home.'

Jacob's Ladder

Soon after our London trip was the day of the tea for poor children. The people of Lees baked and made potted meat and jellies, and when the day came, Mother, the Aunts, Miss Carter and lots more ladies made a most delicious tea. The children and mothers arrived in wagonettes, then a lorry brought the Parson, Mr Green (the new Curate), some more men, and a lady to play the harmonium, and the service began. One poor little girl cried – she wanted her tea: she'd had no dinner. At one tea, Great-Aunt Jane said, 'God felt sorry for the children having to wait so long, so he propped the two halves of Jacob's ladder against each end of a pink cloud. "Hey, children," he said, "up you go." And up they trooped to the Happy Land, which was like a big bouncy feather bed. What a good time they had: God kept them on the move. "Down you go carefully." When they got to the bottom the people were singing "There is a Happy Land, Far, Far Away". The children laughed, and shouted "We've been, we've been," and, at last tea was ready.'

Jonah and the Whale

Once I dreamed that after we'd walked through the snowy park on our way home the little black island moved and the whale's great head came out of the water near the landing-stage. To our great surprise out walked Jonah dressed in his best clothes. 'Bless me,' said Grandma, 'if you aren't Jonah!' She took his had and seemed very pleased to see him. 'Now you must come back with us and have a cup of tea.' 'Oh Missus, I can't,' he said, 'I've to go and see my people.' 'Where are your people?' asked Grandma. 'They're in Egypt,' he replied. 'But you can't go all that long way without your tea,' said Grandma. But just then the whale wept long and loud because it wanted Jonah to come back and stay with it.

Sunday

On a warm Sunday afternoon Mother, Grandma, The Aunts and Miss Carter (who wore Pink) went for a walk in the park. We met Mrs Hope-Ainsworth with Bertie and Nellie. George and I felt sorry, because she insisted on us going to her house to tea, and the year was 1907.

Monday

On Monday we all got up early, Sarah, who came to help, lit the fire under the wash-boiler in the woodshed, and Mother, Aunt Mary also Sarah, began to wash all our clothes, they had to be mangled rinsed and starched, then hung on the lines to dry. What a hard day it was, and the year was 1907.

Tuesday

On Tuesday, Mother took George and I up the hill to Springhead to have tea with Great-Aunt Jane. She told us the lovely story about God who had come to live in a shed which we could see out of her window, and the year was 1907.

Wednesday

On Wednesday Mother baked our bread but she baked such a lot of brown flour Aunt Mary came to knead it. Mother made muffins and we ate them hot, with lots of butter and syrup for our tea, and the year was 1907.

Thursday

On Thursday we always went out for a ride in our new trap drawn by Fanny, our strong- minded horse. We always enjoyed our trips, which ended in Grandma and Aunt Mary and Aunt Frances, also Miss Carter (who wore Pink) and Mr Taylor (the Bank Manager) coming to tea, and the year was 1907.

Friday

On Friday, Mother, George and I called for Grandma, the Aunts and Miss Carter (who wore Pink) to go for a ride on the tramcar to Oldham. We always went to the market. Grandma and Miss Carter thought they would buy some lace curtains but George and I liked the man with lots of toys, and the year 1907.

Hurrying Summer – April

This is April and coming home from Great-Aunt Jane's who lived up Springhead, it suddenly began to pour with rain, and it really did rain, but, we'd got to the bottom of the hill, and to the beginning of the houses in Milking Green, so that Mother, Grandma and the Aunts didn't worry because, when the kind lady called to us to come in and shelter, Mother said, 'It is only an April shower and will soon be over, thank you', and there behind us was an April rainbow, and the year was 1907.

Hurrying Summer – May

This is May, and it was our first morning at Grandpa's in Blackpool
and it was a lovely morning, so Miss Carter (who wore Pink) said,
'Let us go to the farm for the milk,' but when we got near to the farm,
Miss Carter, Mother and the Aunts wondered if the cows had been let
out to the fields, but, just in front of us was the farmers boy with his
dog, so we were safe, and the year was 1907.

Hurrying Summer – June

This is June, and a lovely warm evening. 'Instead of you and George going to bed, we'll go for a walk and just have a look at the Tower and the sea,' said Mother. And there was the Tower and the sea in the distance, but, on a low branch in front of us was a blackbird singing his song of love and joy, and the year was 1907.

Hurrying Summer – July

This is July, and, oh what joy, to walk out of Grandpa's gate into the Enchanted Garden, and this evening George and I saw something we had never seen before – dragonflies. We were just a little afraid of them at first, but Mother and the Aunts just laughed and said, 'they won't bite or hurt you, they must have come from the pond and just look how lovely they are,' and the year was 1907.

Hurrying Summer – August

This is August, warm and mellow, and Grandpa saying, 'Come along, get your hats on, and we'll all go and see the miller at Martin Mill.' Off we all went in the dog cart pulled by Prince so whilst Grandpa talked to the miller and Mother, the Aunts and Miss Carter (who wore Pink) looked to see how the blackberries were ripening. George and I played amongst the stooks of golden corn, and the year was 1907.

Hurrying Summer – September

This is September, and our last Saturday evening at Blackpool, so Mr Taylor wanted to see the last cricket match at Wrea Green. Miss Carter (who wore Pink) always pretended she loved cricket, but Mother, the Aunts, George and I found it boring, so we gathered blackberries to take back with us to Oldham. Oh how sad to leave Blackpool but it will be rather nice to see all our friends again, and the year was 1907.

Miss Carter

Mother

Every Friday Evening Maggie Knott Told Us How Her Brother Harry Died for His Country

Often we went with Aunt Mary to visit Maggie Knott and take her a little of something that Grandma had to spare. Sometimes it was home-cured bacon or a brown dish of fresh butter, but it was always the same story we had to sit and listen to – How poor Harry was killed by a canon ball while defending his Queen and country. All her life Maggie had been a handloom weaver and would go to people's houses weaving their sheets. She was now very old and, as she said, looking forward to the day when she would behold Harry in his scarlet coat, seated at the Right Hand of God, and the year was 1906.

Great-Aunt Helen

Great-Aunt Helen, who left me her Bible.

We Looked Forward to Tuesday

We looked forward to Tuesday afternoons with delight and were always eager to be off to Springhead to listen to Great-Aunt Jane telling another episode of the doings of God; but, alas, she fell asleep. Mother said, 'Hush, she will soon wake – it is only a little cat-nap.'

Mother and Helen with Dog

Queen Alexandra

Miss Carter and Mr Taylor went off to the Town Hall, Manchester to see the King and Queen step from their carriage and enter. Miss Carter had a good view of the Queen standing against a background of trees and flowers.

Queen Alexandra

Queen Alexandra taking my little cup and saucer.

Henrietta Broken Down

Father bought a new car in 1912. She was very smart and much bigger than the Green Renault which we had in 1909. Esmeralda was a Grey T Ford. She didn't break down like Elija, so on Saturdays we set off to lots of nice places. This Saturday we set off to find Delamere Forest, then on to Chester, but just before we found the main road we had to stop for there in the lane was 'Henrietta', broken down, and also waiting to pass was a large beautiful Rolls Royce. 'Oh, isn't he beautiful, I'm sure he's called Sir William,' but Sir William's owners were not pleased at having to wait until Henrietta's works were repaired, so Mother got out our picnic things and made a nice tea. Mother asked someone to take Sir William's owners a nice cup of tea for which they were thankful and were really very nice when we got to know them, and the year was 1915.

It was a Beautiful Place

It was a beautiful place, and always on our homeward journey from Blackpool, Father would stop the car and allow us to look at the lovely wide river, and bank of trees now clothed in their new spring green. As well as the river, there were beautiful carriages with high-stepping horses and ladies dressed in the height of fashion. There were nursemaids with children in fancy bassinets. Mother, Aunt Frances, and Miss Carter (who wore Pink), took off their dust coats, which ladies had to wear to protect their clothing against the weather and the dust off the roads. Whilst we enjoyed the scene, Father guarded the car, as horses, if they got the chance, would kick it, or if they got the bit between their teeth, would bolt at the sight of it. Such was the exciting year 1909.

The Red Parasol

'Oh dear, I wish those cows would go home. Please Father can we go
quicker,' but Father was getting cross and said that people had no
right to let their hens wander in the road. Then Mother said she knew
what to do. She had her new red silk parasol in the car and if she
opened it and waved it at them they would be frightened and go
away. We had been on our first run into Cheshire with our new car
(it was called Eliza), and the year was 1909.

Friday Night Along Lees Road

Walking home along Lees Road on Friday night was always great fun, especially when it was cold and frosty and dark, because all the shops were lit up and full of nice things. The fish and chips smelled delicious, so did the confectioners next door with their fresh bread, hot muffins, and hot pies. Sometimes they made potato pies in brown basins. They had a crispy crust, and when Mother and the Aunts bought them, we had to hurry home because they were piping hot and looked so good that George and I danced all the way home. When Mr Taylor (the Bank Manager) came to meet Miss Carter (who wore Pink) they always took home something good to eat, but we all felt a little sorry for the poor people who were flitting with their few bits of furniture on a little cart. It was such a cold night, and the year was 1906.

Evening Market Scene

The Church and Chapel Going Home on Sunday Evening

This was a special Sunday – We were all going to Alice Ann's new home to eat a piece of her wedding cake and wish her happiness for only the day before she had become the wife of widower Jim Wilson. Walking along in the picture is – firstly Uncle John, Aunt Annie and Cousin Phyllis, next is Alice Ann, in her new blue coat and hat, her new husband and his four little boys. Behind is Grandfather and Grandmother, next Father and Mother, George and I (and the dogs Gyp and Barney). Then Aunt Mary (in a fashionable sailor hat) and Aunt Frances, Miss Carter (who wore Pink) was walking with them when she hears Mr Taylor (the Bank Manager and also a widower) hurrying along and asks him to accompany them to Alice Ann's, and the year was 1906.

Going Home Through Alexandra Park

Going home through Alexandra Park on a winter evening, George and I, Mother, Grandma and the dogs had gone to meet Aunt Frances and Aunt Charlotte in the park. They had already met Miss Carter, and the three ladies were skating along when they saw Mr Taylor. 'How kind dear Mr Taylor is,' said Mother to Grandma. 'But look, isn't that the Reverend Albert Green walking across the ice towards Charlotte – she is turning towards him. I wonder if anything will come of it.' But George and I had something much more interesting to think about; all the ducks came across the ice asking for food, all the Japanese lanterns were lit, and everything looked like Fairyland.

The Cricket Match

It was a lovely warm early May evening and our first Saturday at Blackpool. Mr Taylor had arrived and so had Father. Mr Taylor suggested we had an early tea, then we would all go to Wrea Green. 'Oh,' said Mother, 'I know why he wants to go to Wrea Green, I do believe the cricket's started.' Well, it was such a nice evening, we all set off, and, sure enough the match was going well, but Mother, the Aunts and even Miss Carter got very tired, and George and I got bored. There were no seats for the ladies to sit on and just when everyone was getting ready to tell Mr Taylor that they thought it was time to go home, some cows got in amongst the match and we had to run behind some trees until someone shoo'd them away, and the year was 1908.

The Fair at Daisy Nook

The Fair at Daisy Nook was a most exciting day, and for weeks George and I looked forward to the day when we packed our picnic hamper, called for Grandma and the Aunts and Miss Carter (who wore Pink), and started on our journey to Failsworth by tramcar. Then we had a good walk along a shady lane to Red Bills and the Fair. This year there was a Fat Lady and some Scots girls who danced a reel to the bagpipes. We didn't go on the roundabout because it made George sick, nor did we go near to the inn because there were a lot of rough men who fought each other. Mr Taylor (the Bank Manager) came later and escorted us round the gypsy caravans and the coconut shies, and the year was 1908.

Grandpa Took Us Through Shudehill Market

Grandpa took us through Shudehill Market to find Prince and the big trap, which we had left in charge of a boy, but Grandma, the Aunts, Mother, George and me, also Miss Carter (who wore Pink) didn't like the place. There were cages of hens and sometimes a man would drag one out and kill it, but, while Mother was trying to get George and I away, Grandpa rushed up to a man who was beating a poor sad donkey. He ordered him to stop and said he would buy the poor creature, so Neddy came home with us in the trap and was much loved, and the year was 1906.

Hollinwood Market

For a special treat we all went to Hollinwood Market. Mother, George and I called for Grandma and the Aunts, also Miss Carter (who wore Pink). She and Grandma thought they would look at the stall selling lace curtains, but George and I saw a man with a basketful of lovely toys. We were so delighted we let go the dogs' leads, but Gyp and Barney didn't run away. Mother was cross, she said toys were for birthdays and Christmas, and the year was 1906.

Mill on Fire

'Fire! Fire!' everyone cried. Mother, George and I and the dogs, Gyp and Barney, left the two Aunts and Miss Carter (who wore Pink), at the big 'Votes for Women' meeting at the Town Hall. There was a lot of shouting and the Police were wondering what to do because the women wouldn't let the trams pass. So Mother took us away to a quieter part of the town, but when we saw the big railway warehouse on fire, we were rather afraid because we had to pass it on our way to the park and home, and the year was 1908.

The Mill Yard

'Children,' said Great-Aunt Mary, 'Would you like to look at the big boiler fires?' 'Oh yes please,' said George and I. So Aunt Mary, took us into the mill yard and we warmed our hands at the flowing fires. Mother, Grandma, Aunt Mary, Aunt Frances and Miss Carter (who wore Pink) had been up Springhead to visit Great-Aunt Jane. Today we were rather late going home and got caught up in the rush of people coming out of the County End Mill so George and I could only have a peek at the big mill fires. Mr Taylor (the Bank Manager) is meeting us and we were all going to Grandma's for tea, and the year was 1907.

Tarporley Races

One fine summer's day, Grandpa gave us a treat. We all went to Tarporley Races. Even Miss Carter came, and so did Mr Taylor. There we met Mrs Hope-Ainsworth with Bertie and Nellie, a dreadful girl who spent her time listening to other people's conversation. Then she would tell her Mother, especially if she thought any of the ladies of Lees fancied their Bertie. We only saw one race because Fanny and Prince thought they ought to join in, which quite frightened Mother, Grandma and the Aunts. There were lots of drunken men and we saw one man running away with a bag of money. Even Mr Taylor gave chase, shouting, 'Stop thief.'

'Oh Dear', Said Mother

'Oh dear,' said Mother, 'Those poor horses are being taken to Mumps Station and then off with the soldiers to France, I do believe they know. I'm sure the one in the cart is telling the big black one all about it.' Mother, Aunt Mary, Miss Carter (who wore Pink) and Mr Taylor (the Bank Manager) came into the town to meet me, and to see if there was a little cheese or butter to spare in the shops. 'Just let me pat this lovely little grey,' I said to the young soldier, holding him. 'Isn't he a beauty,' he said, 'I'll look after him Miss.' 'Please do,' I said, 'I hope you will all come back safely to Oldham – this war seems as though it will never end,' and it is now September 1917.

The Zeppelins

It was a quiet moonlight night in early winter, and I thought how peaceful it was as I hurried along into the town to attend my evening class in embroidery. The students were all quiet and busy working, when suddenly all the lights went out, and there was a roaring noise coming nearer. Everyone immediately rushed for the street, and there, quite low, were three Zeppelins. The first one had just gone ahead, but the other two were so low we felt sure we could hit them if only we had something. The searchlights lit them up as they slowly roared overhead. The special policeman with his bike, talking to me, tried to make all the students go back into the school, but we felt we had to see what was happening. That was the only time the Zeppelins ever got so far north. They did drop their bombs near Bolton, and the year was 1917.

I Always Looked at the Map in the Newsagents

It was always sad to see the little red flags on the map in the newsagent's shop in Lees Road. I always got off the tram there so that I could see how near to Paris the war had got and as I looked each week it seemed as though the war would never end. Life was very hard for all of us. There was no time now for holidays, it was always work! And the year was 1916.

Thank Goodness There's a Policeman

Thank goodness there's a policeman. He was a wartime policeman but I was glad to know he'd help me if I called, but usually, on my way home from work, there was nothing but dark streets, and I used to think I could hear someone padding along behind me. Every night I carried home the day's takings in a brown Gladstone bag and it was mainly gold sovereigns – they were very heavy and all through those dark winter nights, I was always glad to see home and to know I was safe, and the year was 1915.

The War did Not End at Christmas

The war did not end at Christmas as everyone had hoped, so Father said that we'd better get off quick to Blackpool to see Grandpa before petrol got scarce, but, just as we were turning out of Oldham Road into Piccadilly we saw Uncle John and family driving past in his new Dodge. Uncle John saw us and pulled up in front of Lewis's and waited for Father. Father's face got redder and redder and when we pulled up next to Uncle John, Father and he had a frightful row. Uncle John said he was going to Blackpool also. Father said he wasn't, because we couldn't all stay with Grandpa. However Uncle John, Aunt Josephine and our three young cousins got rooms nearby, and in spite of Father's bad temper, we all enjoyed ourselves, and the year was spring 1915.

My First Day at Work

In March 1915 our traveller was called up. Father arrived home distraught. 'I am beginning to think we shall have to close our business,' he said. Then he saw me, 'First thing tomorrow you start work, you will need a much longer skirt and good tweed jacket.' The next day I took over a horse called Gertie and started on my travels. Father said I was to go to Middleton, and Gertie knows all the shops and streets so off you go, but I still hadn't found Middleton and it was twelve o'clock. Me, Gertie, the trap full of parcels were all lost. Luckily I found a policeman, 'Well Miss, you're a tidy way off, but turn right and keep on.' How hard we all worked, and although everyone said the war would be over by Christmas – it went on and on – the year was 1915.

Gathering Blackberries [Stage 1 and 2]

It is interesting to see, from the different stages shown here, how Helen Bradley worked. The completed painting is opposite.

Gathering Blackberries

It was our last day at Blackpool before going back to Lees, near Oldham. It was a beautiful warm September day. Mother said, 'Why not let us gather a basketful of blackberries to take back with us.' Soon Aunt Frances, Aunt Mary, Miss Carter (who wore Pink) and Mr Taylor (the Bank Manager) were ready and off we went into the sunshine. Mother was busy filling her basket, but George and I saw a game of cricket starting, so off we went to watch it. Mr Taylor saw it also and he quite forgot Miss Carter, he was in such a hurry to get to it. It being such a lovely day, and our last, Mother and the Aunts felt sure he would propose to her, but he didn't, and the year was 1909.

Gathering Blackberries

It was our last afternoon at Blackpool, so Mother said, 'Let us go gathering blackberries in the Enchanted Garden. We'll take them back with us tomorrow, along with all the apples Grandpa got from St Michaels,' so our last afternoon at Blackpool was a very happy one, except for the thought that we had to say goodbye to our pond, and the little moorhens and the lovely Enchanted Garden. 'But never mind George, when we get back home to Lees, it will soon be Christmas with that little horse you want, then, after Christmas it will be spring and Grandpa's and Blackpool again', and the year was 1906.

Our Picnic

The sun was going down on a beautiful autumn day. Aunt Mary has started to pack away the picnic things as Grandpa has gone to look to the horses. It was the last picnic of the summer, so Uncle John and Aunt Josephine and the little cousins had come with us, and as we all walked together towards Grandpa, with Prince, and the wagonette and our Fanny in the trap and Uncle John's dogcart with Zober, everyone sang, 'Now the day is over, stars begin to peep, birds and beasts and flowers, soon will be asleep.' And soon George and I were asleep, nestling against Grandma, and the year was 1906.

Bringing the Blackberries Home

Bringing the blackberries home after our last walk through the Enchanted Garden. We were going home to Lees in the morning and we were taking the blackberries back with us to make jam and jelly. We were also taking back two barrels of apples from Grandpa's garden, a home-cured ham for the winter which would soon be upon us when we got back. Mr Taylor (the Bank Manager) had walked on to meet us and, 'Dear me,' said Aunt Mary. 'Just look what a fuss he is making of Miss Carter (who wore Pink) as though she couldn't carry that little basket of blackberries,' and the year was 1907.

Buying Ducks for Christmas

Mother said it wouldn't be long before it was Christmas and that we'd better be thinking about ducks! Grandpa was coming to stay with us for a few days, and Grandpa loved duck. So, although it had snowed through the night, the Aunts and Miss Carter (who wore Pink) called for Mother, George and I, and decided to go up to Warfe's Farm and see if they had any ducks. When we arrived there, Annie Warfe was feeding the hens, and, there quacking along in a line were the ducks, so Mother asked if they could let us have four, and they arrived in time for Grandpa and all of us to have a good dinner, and the year was 1906.

Our Christmas Ducks

Grandpa liked duck for his Christmas dinner which meant that we had to saddle up Prince and go to a farm at Pilling near Fleetwood. Ducks, said Grandpa, always had to live near fresh water, so George and I loved the little stream with all the ducks and little fishes. But Mother was always glad when we were safely back in the little wagonette along with six ducks packed in a basket – all ready to roast for our dinner, and the year was Christmas 1908.

The Afternoon of Christmas Day

Father Christmas came along the promenade on the afternoon of Christmas Day. George and I were just in time to see the beautiful white circus horses coming along in their scarlet trappings and there was Father Christmas with his fairies who threw small pieces of Blackpool Rock in twists of paper for the children. Grandpa, old Mr Bickerstaff, Mr Taylor (the Bank Manager) and Miss Carter (who wore Pink) came with us, but Mr Taylor was so anxious to be nice to Miss Carter, that he would have missed it had not Aunt Charlotte prodded him. Oh, what a happy day it was, and the year was 1907.

Going Home Through the Park

We were caught in the first snow of Winter and Mother who hadn't brought her umbrella wouldn't wait for George and I to feed the ducks. 'Come along quickly children' she called. Poor Miss Carter (who wore Pink) was wearing her new winter dress and hat, never dreaming it would snow, and Miss Maitland and her mother walking in front of her were delighted to see Mr Taylor (the Bank Manager) hurrying towards them to offer his umbrella, and the year 1907.

Gathering Ivy

Policeman in Snow

Christmas Eve was Bright and Clear

Christmas Eve was bright and clear, so Mother said that George and I could go with the Aunts, Miss Carter, Mr Taylor, Mrs Maitland and Dear Emily to join the carol singers down Milking Green. We were just in time to sing 'Christians Awake', which everyone sang lustily. We ended with 'Let there be Light'. The fields and trees were shining white in the light of the moon, and there was light, for Love came down at Christmas, and the year 1908 had almost ended.

John Henry Came on Sunday

John Henry always came to dinner on Sundays. He always said
Grace which was a lengthy sermon, it cooled down our food and
upset Aunt Mary by causing her delicious Yorkshire pudding to go
flat. George is getting ready to cry, and the year was 1906.

Father Said That I Had to Play the Blue Bells of Scotland

Father said that I had to play the Blue Bells of Scotland, but, Oh dear, I couldn't with Father standing next to me and beating time with his violin bow, so I closed my eyes and started, but Father saw I wasn't looking at the music and was cross. George came to my rescue – he insisted on pomping very loud on the bass notes, and said that he'd cry if he couldn't play, so Mother said that she would lift me down and I could try again another time. We were glad Mr Taylor (the Bank Manager) and Miss Carter (who wore Pink) had come along with Grandma and the Aunts to spend the evening with us, and the year was 1906.

'Oh Dear,' Said Aunt Frances

After we'd all seen the Queen, a new magazine came to be sold. The Queen, so it informed us, now wore the long straight sleeves – all the puckers and gathers had gone out of fashion. There was also an advertisement for the new face powder; it would be sent in a plain wrapper. Then the Aunts found what they wanted – new curling tongs, so off Miss Carter went to Manchester to buy them. Aunt Frances was going out to tea with her new young man, so Aunt Mary said she would try them out on her. Aunt Mary heated the tongs and Mother read the instructions and Miss Carter made some tea. Then Aunt Mary clamped the tongs on Aunt Frances's hair. My, it sizzled and a bit fell out, but when it was curled and piled up like Queen Alexandra's, she looked beautiful. And when Mother saw her go with her young man, she said that she was sure he would propose to her, but Aunt Frances wouldn't accept, because I heard Mother say that she really liked James Alfred, our chemist, and the year was 1905.

Going Through the Enchanted Garden

We walked through the Enchanted Garden to the farm because Grandpa said he would like chicken for dinner, so he said, 'Come along Ladies and get your hats on, and see if the farmer has any nice plump chickens.' It was a lovely spring morning with the wild cherries covered in blossom. The Aunts called for Mr Taylor and Miss Carter to come with us, also, much to our surprise, Mrs Maitland said, 'Come along Emily, we'll go also.' There was just the pond which worried Mother. She had to watch George because he loved water and would be in it if she didn't keep an eye on him. George and I had been watching the pond to see if the frogs had arrived, and much to our surprise, there they were but alas, we'd forgotten our jam jars, and the year was 1907.

Going Through the Woods

We had very few places near Lees or Oldham where there were trees with walks through them, but, by taking a tramcar we could have a very nice country walk. We had just arrived back from our long summer holiday at Blackpool with Grandpa. Mother said, 'Let us go round to Grandma's and see if the Aunts won't put their hats on, and come for a walk.' Miss Carter (who wore Pink) and Mr Taylor (the Bank Manager), the Aunts, and even Grandma thought it a good idea and sent George and I round to collect Emily Maitland, who was delighted to come for a walk with us. Much to our surprise, George and I saw a rabbit – much to the delight of Gyp and Barney, and the year was 1907.

Waiting for Grandpa

On Friday afternoons we went with Grandpa to the farm in St Michael's. Grandpa liked to visit the farmer and he bought apples, eggs and home-cured ham. Mother, the Aunts, Miss Carter (who wore Pink) and Mr Taylor (the Bank Manager) also George and I, and sometimes Mrs Maitland and Emily, liked to walk along the path besides the river. Mother said that if we walked along the path we were safe from cows, but, 'Oh dear, whatever shall we do,' cried Miss Carter, 'Just look at those cows, how ever shall we get past them,' but Mr Taylor said, 'Come along, I've got my stick and we'll be alright.' Mother said, after we were safely past the cows, 'I don't know whatever we would do without Mr Taylor, he's so very kind,' and the year was 1906.

Outing

Family in Spring Lane

It was our last walk along Spring Lane before setting off for Blackpool the next morning. Grandma, the Aunts and Miss Carter (who wore Pink) called for us and, as they walked along talking about all the little things they had to do before the cabs came the next morning, Willie and Annie Murgatroyd came running up to George and I, Annie saying that they would see us at the station the next morning as they were going to their auntie's at Blackpool. 'What's the matter with Willie,' said Grandma. 'He's got the mumps,' shouted Annie. 'Oh dear me,' said Mother, 'that's the last straw. Children, put your hankies to your noses.' 'I've never had the mumps,' said Miss Carter, 'and look, Mr Taylor (the Bank Manager) is coming. Let us all turn back quickly', and the year was 1908.

Going Home

It was a Beautiful April Evening

It was a beautiful April evening, and too early for George and me to go to bed, so Mother said, 'Don't let us stay indoors, let us go into the Enchanted Garden, and look at the wild cherry blossom, it will soon be over.' So we put on our hats, and the Aunts and Miss Carter collected their scissors to cut bunches of sweet-scented narcissus flowers to take back to their lodgings. Mr Taylor and Father had gone out for the evening, and Miss Carter gathered an extra bunch to give to Mr Taylor's landlady, so that she would be extra kind to him.

Bulls Outside Buckley & Proctor

On Fridays Mother, George and I, the Aunts, and sometimes, Grandma, also Miss Carter, used to enjoy going to Oldham. That meant the Market, but sometimes we got no further than Buckley & Procter's shop at Mumps Bridge. This Friday we were looking at the shop windows when there was a frightful noise and round the corner came a wild looking bull. Everyone rushed through the shop door, except Aunt Mary, who opened the umbrella straight in the face of that bull, but more of them rushed round the corner so Aunt Mary pulled down the umbrella and dashed for the door just in time, and the year was 1908.

Driving Out with Fanny

Driving out with Fanny, she took a dislike to the new circular manhole covers in the road and took a flying leap over them. Miss Carter (who wore Pink) saw the shocking spectacle, so also did Mr Taylor, the Bank Manager and Mrs Austin Jenkinson (the year 1906).

Friday Afternoon at the Co-op

On Friday afternoons, Mother, Aunt Frances, Aunt Mary, Miss Carter (who wore Pink) and George and I walked quite a long way to a new Co-operative Stores to buy our flour to bake our bread. The first time we went to the shop we saw little boys hurrying to the shop from school – it was to buy the flour and carry it home in pillowcases on their heads – nearly all the mothers baked their bread on Saturdays and if Aunt Frances took George and I and Gyp and Barney for a walk on Saturdays, the delicious smell of home-baked bread always made us hungry. The special flour that was sold in the Stores was from their own flour mill and was unbleached, and when it was baked it gave us 'The Golden Loaf'. On my twelfth birthday mother said, 'Now you're twelve you must take over the bread baking,' so every Saturday morning I stoked up the fire oven and got on with the job of providing ourselves with seven two-pound loaves, and the year was 1912.

Foden Steam Wagon

'Oh,' said mother, 'Look at Gertie, she's taken fright, I do hope that man can hold her steady until that frightful steam engine gets past that tram.' Father and I were returning to our warehouse after delivering goods and hoping to finish early when we heard Mother's voice, and there she was with the Aunts and Miss Carter (who wore Pink). They were going to look at Baileys Pot Shop. Father, along with all the other people who owned horses, was very annoyed at the Government allowing the new Sentinel Steam Wagon on the highway. He was so cross he wrote to Winston Churchill about it, but alas, it didn't stop them, and the year was 1915.

I Went to Shannons for Butter

A woman hurried past Mother and called to her, 'They've got butter at Shannons.' 'Quick,' called Mother to me. 'Get your hat on and go along to see if they'll let you have some. Goodness, I don't care if it's only a quarter of a pound.' Butter and even Margarine had become very scarce. 'Oh, and see if they'll let you have anything else.' How I hurried along the two miles to Oldham, and what a long queue there was, but joy oh joy, I got half a pound and ran all the way back home, and the year was 1916, and the war seemed as if it would never end.

Going to Bailey's Pot Shop

Sometimes on Friday afternoons Mother, George and I, with Grandma, the Aunts, and Miss Carter (who wore Pink), walked through Glodwick to visit Great-Aunt Buckley. She, like Great-Aunt Jane, lived in a big dark house, and like her, was very strict. We had to sit still on her sofa and be good, but sometimes she would let us play in the kitchen. There was always Polly, her maid, sitting before the fire. She had a big cat called Joe who loved to play hide and seek with us. Polly made delicious parkin, and George and I always had a lump before going home, but today we didn't go straight home through the park, but up into Oldham, to Bailey's Pot Shop because, alas, Mother only just remembered in time that tomorrow was Mrs Maitland's birthday, and we had promised to get her a cream jug, so we bought her a lovely one with pink roses all over it, and the year was 1906.

Bonnie Warfe

We all loved Bonnie Warfe, the milk horse. She stood in the street patiently waiting until everyone had their milk jugs filled, then Annie or Jimmy Warfe would climb in the milk float, look at George and I and call to Mother, 'Can these two come round with us?' Mother would laugh and say, 'Very well, if you can put up with them.' So up we got and away Bonnie went until we got to the next stop, and life was good in the year 1907.

We Set Out to Visit Great-Aunt Buckley

We set out to visit Great-Aunt Buckley, 'and,' said Mother, 'everybody seems to be spring cleaning.' There was Mrs Ormrod with a line full of washing, and Minnie and Poor Little Sammy were out with her in the sunshine. Everyone felt sorry for Poor Little Sammy, he was so white and thin and always ailing. Grandma, Mother and Aunt Frances are talking to him, but Aunt Mary has seen John Sam'el's chimney on fire and John Sam'el calmly watching it. How angry all the women are, 'Just when we've got all our washing on the line, he always does this,' and they shouted at him, but it made no difference, he just stood calmly smoking his pipe and saying nothing. Miss Carter (who wore Pink) had walked on to meet Mr Taylor (the Bank Manager) and was cross also – she was afraid of the soot spoiling her new dress, and the year was 1908.

Oh Jane

On Our Way Home

On our way home from visiting Great-Aunt Jane who lived in Springhead we always passed the chemist shop at County End so that Aunt Frances could stop and have a word with James Alfred, the nice young son of the owner. I heard Mother say to Aunt Mary that she was sure they were in love with one another, but his mother had said he wasn't to dream of marrying, at least not whilst she was alive, so poor James Alfred couldn't call at Grandma's and ask Aunt Frances to walk out with him, so George and I used to run to his shop with little notes which we took round the back. Then he would give us one to take back to Aunt Frances and along with the note a big lump of sugar candy, and the year was 1907.

It was a Warm Day When We Met in Manchester

It was a warm day when we met in Manchester. Mother, George and I, Grandma and the two Aunts had just arrived outside the Royal Infirmary on Piccadilly when Miss Carter arrived with Mr Taylor. Everyone thought it so kind of him to accompany us to Affleck & Brown's to buy a carpet. George and I would have loved to stay with the pigeons, but the shopping had to be done. We did stop to buy some delicious Ashton-Moss celery, though, and Grandma bought some daffodils. Miss Carter lingered near the roses, but Mr Taylor gave all his attention to Grandma. There was a man lying on a bench and a letter boy called to a nurse, 'Please come, I'm sure he's dead.' We hurried away.

The Flood

Once when I must have eaten too much tea I dreamed that it rained and rained until the Square in Lees was a lake with little waves. 'Oh, Grandma, what shall we do?' I asked. 'Well, my dear,' said Grandma, 'don't you remember God promised there would never be another Flood? We've just had a bad storm and the drains won't take all the water. We'll have to get our kitchen tables.' We up-ended all we could get and launched them like boats. Willie Murgatroyd tied the tablecloth to the legs of their table; it made a splendid sail. And he brought his fishing rod and fished. Mr and Mrs Smith brought their little round table and sat eating their tea, and Mrs Hope-Ainsworth, and Bertie and Nellie and the dogs, floated along on their red sofa, which Aunt Mary said would get damp. Then the rain stopped and the water drained away: it had been fun.

Helen Bradley's Last Painting

This oil painting was on Helen Bradleys easel when she died. It gives an insight into the way she worked.June D. Allan, Dronfield,

Derbyshire
Frances Andrews, Westhoughton, Lancashire
Alan Aubrey, Southport
Michael W. Baxter, Rochdale, Lancashire

Subscribers

Peter Bradley, son of Helen Bradley, and family in England and

   Finland

Sylvia I. Bradshaw, West Kirby, Wirral

Pam and Peter Brocklehurst, Oldham, Lancashire

Amelia Charlotte Elizabeth Buckley, Saddleworth, Lancashire

Patrick James Buckley, Saddleworth, Lancashire

Edward James Buckley, Saddleworth, Lancashire

Huelwen Burton, Dwygyfylchi, North Wales

 C C Art Ltd, Wigan, Lancashrie

Brenda Catlow, Clayton-Le-Moors, Lancashire

Christine and Ivor Cheadle, Bolton, Lancashire

Neal and Sarah Cheadle, Tonbridge, Kent

John and Sandra Christian, Kings Gallery, Canterbury

Lucy Clarke, Great Grandaughter of Helen Bradley

Edward Clarke, Great Grandson of Helen Bradley

Victoria Clarke, Great Grandaughter of Helen Bradley

Jean and Michael Clarke, Grandaughter of Helen Brandley

Michael and Wendi Cragg, Blackrod

Eric Davies, Salterforth, Lancashire

Jean Dawson, Poulton-Le-Fylde, Lancashire

Mrs Kathleen Deakin, Lostock, Bolton, Greater Manchester

Mr Justin M. Douglas, St Albans, Hertfordshire

Lauren Eaves, St Albans, Hertfordshire

Christine Eaves, Inglewhite, Lancashire

Lynne R. Ferster

Mrs H.J. Foster, Blackpool, Lancashire

Diana M.K. Furber, Husbands Bosworth, Leicestershire

Riverside Gallery, High Street, Uppermill, Saddleworth, Oldham

Teresa Gaskell, Wigan, Lancashire

Edward T.F. Gauld, Wroughton, Wiltshire

Ginnie, August 2002

Jean Green, Farington Moss, Lancashire

Shelagh Griffiths, Bolton, Lancashire

Anne Griffiths, Tipton, West Midlands

David J. Grimes, Formby, Lancashire

Victoria K. Grimes, Formby, Lancashire

F. Philippa Hargreaves, Croft, Cheshire

Jacqueline Harrison, Whixall, Shropshire

Margaret Hart, Manchester

Dorothy V. Hill, Netherton, Newton Abbot, Devon

Jack and Irene Hirst, Oldham, Lancashire

Roy and Kay Hirst, Rochdale, Lancashire

Helena M. Hodge, formerly of Lancashire

Jean Holland, Silverdale, Lancashire

Rosemary E. Howard, Southport

Samuel Howarth, Saddleworth, Oldham

Dee Johnson, Kendal

Cynthia J. Jones, Wotton-Under-Edge, Gloucestershire

Tim and Donna Joyce, Redditch, Worcestershire

Carol A. Lancaster, Longton, Preston, Lancashire

Barbara and David Layfield and family, niece and great cousin of

    Helen

Casey Lee, St Peter Port, Guernsey

Oliver Lee, St Peter Port, Guernsey

Christina M. Leigh-Baker, Prestwich, Manchester

Ellen Lilley, Seaford, East Sussex

Mrs Sheila Littlewood, Saddleworth, Lancashire

Sylvia Lloyd, Cleveleys, Lancashire

Christine Lowry, Malton, North Yorkshire

Ray Lynden, St Annes, Lancashire

Judith Malkin, Southport

Helen W. Marsh, Bolton, Lancashire

Mr and Mrs R. Matthewman, Pleasington, Lancashire

Patricia McKenna, Bury, Lancashire

Stephen Morton, Grandson of Helen Bradley

Maureen Moss, Claughton 'on' Brock, Preston, Lancashire

Philip H. Mountford, Orwell, Cambridgeshire

Matt J. Newing, Burscough, Lancashire

C.M. Nuttall, Holcombe, Lancashire

Doreen O'Connor, Middleton, Lancashire

Patricia Owen, Rochdale, Lancashire

S.M. Partridge, Ramsbottom, Lancashire

Alison V. Peacock, Leyland, Lancashire

Harold and May Renney, Blackburn, Lancashire

Janice and Bob Rust, Littlebury, Essex

Margaret Salter, Llandudno

Ian and Janet Sandiford, Rochdale, Lancashire

Margaret and Lional Scott, Grange-Over-Sands, Cumbria

Philip Smith, Upholland, Lancashire

Mrs Mavis Smith, Adelaide, South Australia

Mrs Margaret Elaine Smith, Tottington, Bury, Lancashire

Leonard Steinberg

Jonathan Steinberg

Mary Stone, Brentwood, Essex

Lorraine Stones, Bolton, Lancashire

Mrs Elsie Stones, Kearsley, Bolton

Mrs E. Stones

Susan R. Sutton, Hessle, Hull, Yorkshire

Judy Taylor, London

Angela Thornber, Woodhead, Ilkley, Yorkshire

Valerie J. Unsworth, Lancaster

Lucy Westhead, St Helens

Deborah J. Whincup, Marshside, Sououthport

Professor Derek Thomas Whiteside, Cambridge/formerly Blackpool

Colin and Elizabeth Whitfield-Clark, Lytham St Annes

Jim Whittaker, Euxton, Lancashire

Jason, Joanne, Samuel, Emily and Bethany Wilcox,

Anne Williams, Lytham, Lancashire

Lynda M. Williams, Westhoughton, Bolton

Kingsley Wood, Lees, Lancashire

Geoffrey Woodhead, Saddleworth, Yorkshire

John and Sylvia Yates, Norwich, Norfolk

Stephen B.L. Yip, Liverpool